POEMS
cleverly adorned
with words
by JOE

I LOVE
YOU
DOLORES
OUR LOVE IS STRONG AS THIS
LEAF IS GREEN
OUR SYMBOL MY DARLING IT
WILL ALWAYS MEAN. 1950
JOSEPH.

Order this book online at www.trafford.com
or email orders@trafford.com

Most Trafford titles are also available at major online book retailers.

Printed in Victoria, BC, Canada.

ISBN: 978-1-4269-2652-5 (sc)

*Our mission is to efficiently provide the world's finest, most comprehensive
book publishing service, enabling every author to experience success.
To find out how to publish your book, your way, and have it available
worldwide, visit us online at www.trafford.com*

Trafford rev. 02/09/2010

 www.trafford.com

North America & international
toll-free: 1 888 232 4444 (USA & Canada)
phone: 250 383 6864 ♦ fax: 812 355 4082

CONTENTS

An Ode To The Bulb..............................56

Ancestors...68

April Fool Joke.....................................45

As You Sit and Read This Poem............9

Back To School and All The Crazies...120

Baseball..39

Bells Toll Ominously, The.....................43

Best Things Are Free...........................71

Birthday Parties, Balloons, Presents...115

Body Parts, My....................................87

Body Parts, An Ode To My...................87

Call Me! I Can't Remember Now........128

Changing Times...................................90

Children Games and Future...................6

Choices...79

Christmas Parade...............................133

Christmas Dream, A.............................82

Christmas Sales, After.........................95

Christmas Gift, Best.............................93

Congratulations Graduate, Linda..........31

Counter Top Siamese............................7

Countryside Fields...............................74

Curiosity..94

Dancing Fingers..................................18

Diet...42

Dreams of Nightmares.......................106

Dreams...100

Dreams..101

Early Morning Sun and Fog....................2

Earth...20

Easter Egg and Its Miracle...................34

Famous Day, Yet Tragic.......................85

Favorite Place....................................102

Fields..74

Fifty Nine Years.....................................4

Fireworks...63

First Day of Spring...............................34

Flying..65

Free Style..80

Ghosts...50

Gleaming Tree......................................71

Good Times..136

Good Friday...35

Guilty or Not Guilty..............................67

Halloween..84

Happy Birthday.....................................30

Hard Luck..66

Hawk In The Park.................................21

Heavy Cross, The.................................69

Homeless Bum, The..............................72

Homeless...72

House Keeper.......................................81

How I Started A Toy Loan Store.........122

How Much Is Too Much?.....................121

I Am The World's Greatest Liar..........112

I Wonder..58

If I Could Fly.......................................125

Insanity or Sanity.................................94

Into The Future.....................................89

Irish, Oh To Be.....................................36

Irish Poem..5

It Ain't Like That No more.....................49

It's Free..130

I'm Always Thinking

   Of Something To Write..................116

Job...?..73

Judgement Day.....................................78

Large Plot of Ground, A......................119

Leap Year..29

Leaves...134

Lonely Word, The..................................15

Lonely Oak Tree, The............................25

Lost In A Dream....................................38

Lost Poem..98

Love...77

Loving You..31

Making up Words..................................16

March Winds...19

Memorial Day, May 30th.......................48

Mighty Wave...64

CONTENTS

Music..52

My Toe and The Rock.........................27

My Favorite Thing..............................54

My Favorite Stars.............................107

My First Day With The Bulb................55

My First Christmas Tree.....................13

My Favorite Summer.........................113

Mysteries, Faces and Noises.............110

Names..75

Nature's Little Sapling.......................76

New Year's Resolutions, My.............23

New Years Eve...................................96

Newly Weds.......................................59

Nice and Bad Teachers.....................86

Old Time Printing.............................109

On The Farm....................................135

Once Upon A Time...........................111

Our Leaf, A Symbol of Love...................1

Our Sun...65

Our Love, Golden and Grand................4

Our Statue of Liberty..........................24

Our Poems...1

Poem A Day, A..................................14

Poem Line In Two Weeks, A...............57

Poem of Ages....................................12

Poetry To Prose................................64

Pony Ride, My First..........................126

Pot Hole, The.....................................33

Presidents' Day, Poem......................32

Purrrr To You.....................................11

Rats...44

Red Bottle, The..................................18

Remembering Valentines Day.............28

Rumors..92

Running Water...................................10

Sammy, The Lookout Cat...................30

Santa Was Here, Ho! Ho! Ho!..............8

Santa's New Herd..............................17

Seasons and Its Changes.....................3

Sex...15

She Was A Beautiful Cat.....................60

Shoot That Bow and Arrow.................20

Some of My Daily Routines................108

Spooks...99

Stealing..124

Stop Raining On My Parade..............123

Strange Odd People...........................41

Strangest Thing, The........................127

Superstition Poem..............................37

Superstition.......................................37

Swim Suits...62

Thanksgiving......................................88

Then and Now...................................118

Things We Used To Do.......................96

Unfortunately, Things
    Fell Apart, Almost Immediately..........47

Tiny Grains of Sand............................52

Tom the Turkey, the Holiday Bird.......132

Toys...42

Two Face People..............................129

Valentines Day Is For Dolores...........104

Voting..61

Watch Your Glasses...........................21

Watches, Clocks, Chimes, Etc.............50

Weather, Showers and Tornado...........46

We're Getting Old...............................53

What If I Did Change Course?.............54

What Is Shame?...................................9

What Important Things In 2009?..........97

What's A G'ma For?...............................5

When I Was A Kid...............................22

When I Found Out I Wasn't Immortal....51

Whiskey and
    Wild Red Indians Halloween...........131

Winkle and Matilda's April Fool...........45

Winter..91

Witch Is Brewing, The.........................83

Write It Down......................................98

Writing A Morning Poem....................107

Zeppelin Passes By, A..........................2

Our Poems

Knowing each other for fifty five years
Our leaf says nineteen fifty,
I think we earned a lot of cheers.
Don't you think that's pretty nifty?

Where did all the years go, my love?
Time goes by so fast you see.
We started with year number one
And now we're up to fifty three.

We have filled the spaces of time with love.
And still it is growing with help from above.
Like a couple of kids, we are always kissing
In our marriage there is nothing missing.

So time will go on,
And we shall see
What's in the future
For you and me.

Our Leaf,
A Symbol of Love

Our leaf came all the way
from Ogdensburgh, N.Y.
Joe sent it as a
Valentine Letter to
Dolores before they
were married in the
year of 1951.

It reads:
"Our love is as strong as this leaf is green.
Our symbol my darling it will always mean."
from Joseph, 1950

A Zeppelin Passes By
My Window

A passing fancy
This giant balloon
Gazing upon the ground
You can hear the
Humming of its sound
As it flies around and around.

A passing fancy
This giant in the sky
Seen with your naked eye
Buzzing around
And making its sound
Kind of proud doing the town.

Early Morning
Sun and Fog

The morning fog was thick and gray
As the sun rose up to break away.

Its grip on the city was a darkened hue
There was no sky with its color of blue.

It softens views with its palates of grays
As the sun tries to force through its rays.

The fog feels fresh and cool to the touch
It just hangs around and doesn't do much.

It will go away as slowly as it came
And is breath taking all the same.

Nature has its ways at best
Now the sun glows in its nest.

Seasons and Its Changes

(This poem was written in 1936 & revised in 2001)

As Rain clouds burst
And lightning glows
It quenches the thirst
And the forest grows.

Billions of droplets becoming rain
Fall to earth without any pain
Moistens its crust with splashing dance
Between sky and earth it is romance.

The warm rains do not last very long
Its just like a passing song
It clings to the earth but doesn't stay
But it will try another day.

But colder weather stops its flow
As winter comes and that is so
Sprinkling its fluffiness we call snow
Turning to ice as we all know.

But a warming trend begins its mark
Excited by a singing lark
Spring flows water to many streams
As the sun casts its mighty beams.

Look above the sky is blue
The sun is out, it shines like new
Winter is gone, it has run away
And summer is here with plenty to say.

My season is short and I won't last
My days are passing by so fast
I stand strong like a forest so tall
But I'll give way to a colorful Fall.

Our Love
"Golden and Grand"
The Test of Time

Married we did without ornaments and frills
As many did with pompous but did not last.
Testing our years of time with all the thrills
We vowed our love, we kept it fast.

Staying together with words of love
Promises were kept by each of us.
Guided our strength from far above
We made it through without fuss.

Saint Valentine, he was our guide,
He was good to us, with his helping hand.
As Cupid flung his arrows with all his pride
It made our love golden, strong & grand.

Our children and families brighten the sky,
Grandchildren, 3 girls, 4 boys & more who knows
What's in store for the future if we think and try
Just imagine, this all started with a leaf and a rose.

59 Years

Fifty nine years of happy days
Together we shared them all
Walking hand and hand
Under sunshine rays
Feeling tall and having a ball.

There are many hearts of red
In this life for you and me
Remember the vow to you I said
"I do and it will last forever, you see."

So my lovely wife on this happy day
We think of all the years
We kept our promises and we can say
Our family was raised with our loving dears.

Irish Poem

Clear as a bell, the sky so 'green',
Most prettiest sight you've seen.
The rainbow flows into its pot o' gold
We seek its fortune so the story's told.
Picking up shamrocks along the way
To bring us luck on this glorious day.
And if you find what you're looking for,
Your dreams will come true,
Thru its open door.

What's A G'ma For?

She's always there for me
And will always be,
My G'ma with a great big smile
And not just once in a while.

She'll rock me to sleep
And in my dreams I'll keep
Her happy face in my mind
And in my heart I shall always find.

My G'ma will share her loving things
So in my life there will be wedding rings
Yes, my G'ma I love you
And I know you love me too!

You give your love to everyone
And when the days are done,
The sunsets followed by sunrises,
Will always bring new surprises!

*With Lots of Love,
from All Your Grandchildren*

Children Games and Future

Children playing games,
It is up to you to guess their names,
They could be any place on earth you see,
The world is their playground that's meant to be.

Boys and girls of many ages
Are the future for mankind,
And you will see as you turn the pages
Happiness and riches are theirs to find.

They are young and so precious to us,
We tend to forget we were there once,
Going through life without any fuss
Mom was there for their noontime lunch.

They will grow up to be good and strong
And proud with their heads up high.
They do their things while singing a song,
Dancing through life as years go by.

Good luck to them, our loving dears.
Grab your future without any fears.
Don't change your ways, hold on fast.
Your heartfelt dreams will forever last.

The Counter Top
Siamese

Up on the counter top
Sammy springs,
To eat her snacks
That mamma brings.

Sometimes she sits
And stares with a glare,
As if to say, "Where's my food,
I'm hungry as a bear."

You see, I'm a Siamese,
I can do anything I please.
So I think I'll take a nap
And cuddle up with ease.

When she awakes
In her eye there a glitter.
She'll run to bathroom
To sit on her litter.

In the dark of night
She'll scamper around
Driving everyone crazy
Just fooling around.

A new day arrives.
"I'm happy as can be,
So we'll start all over,
I'm your pet you see."

Santa Was Here,
Ho! Ho! Ho!

A Christmas Tree is a heart's delight.
Behold, its a most beautiful sight.

With lights aglow and sprinkled with snow
And decorated with garlands high & low.

Young and old will be waiting for him
For his presence will be just a passing whim.

Its meaning of happiness is known throughout
Because there will be presents underneath no doubt.

With his reindeer a'flyin he puts on a show.
Saying to all,"Santa Was Here" "Ho! Ho! Ho!"

As You Sit and Read This Poem

(written just for

As you sit and read this poem
In the comfort of your home,
Think of what I had to do
To get this idea from me to you.

Words, words, that's what they are
All cramped in my head like a jar
Jumping out unscrambled onto this page
Flowing easy and sometimes with rage.

Keep on reading my friend to see
Where this poem is leading me.
If I get stuck here and there.
Please stop me from pulling my hair.

Its Fun to jot this verse from brain
To please the reader is my gain
If you like it, don't utter a sound.
If not my friend, just put it down.

What Is Shame?

"After Eve ate the Apple, in the eyes of God." she later felt shame,
Eating from the "Tree of Knowledge," she knew who to blame.
It was that devious serpent coiled around that tree.
Saying, "Here is a nice juicy red apple grown just for thee."

Running Water

When I first put up my house around 1954 in the country there were no city water pipes laid out in the farmland. So we had to drill for water. 67 feet deep the water driller hit a vein of running spring water about 27 gallons per minute.

That said, we had running water as long as the pump was running & with 4 kids the water pump was always running. In dry seasons the water table dropped & we had to take it easy. We had to let the well recuperate until we could run the water for our needs.

The house was embedded in shale rock. When the rains came we had running water in the cellar. The sump pump was always running. That was a headache.

On rainy days when the electric power was knocked out, we had to bail the water out of the cellar. The whole family participated in this event. They laughed about it.

I finally sold the house and came to California where there is no snow except for the higher elevations. You all know about the water shed from the mountains like Mt. Shasta and other high peaks to supply neighboring communities with water. If you ever go to San Joaquin Valley visit the aqueducts to see how the water is delivered to all neighboring farmlands, towns & cities.

So drink hearty, my friends, there's plenty for all of us.

Purrrr To You...!

Her nose up high as she sniffs the air,
The aroma is great, so she jumps with care.
Up on the counter top she goes
She was right to follow her nose.

Scrumptious foods, oh what a dish,
Especially that wonderful tasty fish.
She eats all day, crunch, crunch, crunch.
"Hey my dish is empty, where's my lunch?"

"Who's got who trained in this house don't you know?
Why it's my masters of course, Dolores & Joe."
Filling her dishes through out the night
Just so Sammy can have a bite.

There's more to this story don't you know,.
"Grroww, not a meow," she yells to Joe.
"It's five in the morning, check out the litter
It's not gold in there Joe, and there's no glitter."

"So cover up my gift to you,
I'm too lazy to follow through,
I'm the pet in this house and I'll have my way,
Guess what guys, tomorrow's another day."

Poem of Ages

Through the ages poems are written,
By people of all walks of life,
Describing experiences with pen in hand,
About life, love ever so grand.
I leave this legacy of "Poems of Ages"
For all to read as we turn the pages.

A child, grandchild or a great-grandchild
Fills the voids of emptiness.
We have waited a generation of time,
But we are happy never the less.
Whether its a boy or girl we don't mind
To give our love happily we confess.

As seasons grow old, we make way for the new,
Giving life on earth as we always do,
Its a wonderful gift from heaven above.
His love is as pure a snow white dove.
But to our children it becomes just a new born day,
Their youth will not last, their just here to play.

My First Christmas Tree Experience (1933)

It was Christmas morning when I visited my Uncle Rock and Aunt Josephine in their living room.

As usual I always go downstairs to visit "Zizzie." That is what I called her. It probably means 'Auntie.'

Not knowing what to expect and what I would find on Christmas morning I didn't say too much. I was excited.

As I entered the living the room I smelled a strong scent of pine. My first impression of a huge decorated Christmas Tree that went up to the ceiling, will forever stay with me.

At the very top was a glowing white angel with a halo.

There were very soft colored lights on the tree glowing steadily. I was all alone in a very still and solemn room.

It was very quiet and breathtaking.

It was daytime and the sun casts its sunbeams on the colored Christmas balls and crystals.

Zizzie always had crystals that were once dangled on a chandelier. She hung them in the window and they made the sun rays dance around the living room. What a sight it was to see the lights and sun beams dance on the walls. There were rainbows and colored lights all over the living room.

I remember a very large blue Christmas ball hanging in front of the tree. As I slowly confronted the sphere, the reflection of my nose on the ball got bigger and bigger, I thought that was funny. I had to try other balls of different sizes. But the blue ball worked the best. Maybe that is why favorite is blue.

The decorations on the tree were ornaments that came from Italy. They were truly old fashion and very delicate. They were handed down from generation to generation.

Every Christmas, even to this day, I still think of my first Christmas tree experience way back in 1933. I was only 5 years old at that time.

A Poem a Day

Adding a line to a poem a day
May be difficult for one to say.
It may be music in verse as we listen
By moonlight our poem will sing and glisten.

Choosing words to make them dance
In our poem they will enhance.
Fitting by rhyme or just line by line
This poem when read will be yours and mine.

Thinking it may end we find more words
Like countless seeds that feed the birds.
It goes on and on with no end in sight
Sewing words together that sounds just right.

Rhyme by rhyme, words as we know,
What does it mean, what does it say?
Our poem has to end and that is so
But we'll write a poem for another day.

The Lonely Word

One word alone may not make sense,
It keeps us in a state of suspense.
It may have meaning just a little bit
So we put different words around it.

Our word may be happy or may be sad
It may be the only meaning it ever had.
One word, one word is what we're looking for,
To make our sentence not be a bore.

Letters, letters make up our hero,
Without them we'll have less then zero.
Now put all our words in a nice straight line
To have a story that will be just fine.

Sex

Discussing Sex between Religion &
Sexual preference is difficult to embark.
Today those in marriage & those who are not,
Governmental laws keep them in the dark.
Whose to say what is wrong or what is right?
Discussions will always end up in a fight.
Your religious ideas are yours to keep.
Your sexual manifestation may make you weep.
So what ever your decision is, it is your right
Hold true to your beliefs with all your might.

Making Up Words

My English may be a little rusty
Or it may be just a little dusty,
I'll put in a word that's kinda' of gutsy,
To make this verse a little lusty.

There just ideas that comes in my head.
When I'm trying to sleep in my bed.
If I put "a" before "b" or "b" before "a"
What in the world am I trying to say?

I'll make up a word that pleases me
Then I'll be happy gosh o' gee.
Be creative my friend and you'll succeed
In making up words that you will need.

Will it be bottle or tottle or just plain mottle
Does that any make sense my friend?
Be creative, make up words and you will see
Your words will take shape, without gosh o' gee.

The above poem
"Making Up Words"
is a prelude to the next poem
"Santa's New Herd"
by Christine,
which appears on next page

Santa's New Herd

by Christine Sachs - inspired by Joe Soldano (Dad)

Have you heard about **Santa's New Herd?**
The North Pole has announced the big word.
What began as a humorous hunch,
Is now Santa's newly horned bunch.

They haven't been sent from Heaven,
And they only number in seven.
Though they are especially bright,
Each deer holds a blessed delight.

Santa chose each one with dubious care,
His reputation is oh, so fair!
They are as follows by selective name,
In which they will claim their moment of fame.

First, there is **Mottle** who has too many spots,
Not contagious, but scratches a lot.
Second is **Rusty** who is sweetened with grace,
Because of arthritis, he must wear a brace.

Then there is **Gutsy** the bravest of all,
He fears nothing being teensy and small.
Gosh O'Gee hiccups and loves a bit of the "nip",
But has never ever failed Santa a sleigh trip!

Dusty is flea bitten and requires some care,
With prodding and hugs, he can sit in a chair.
Tottle bestows a great Dickens's name,
Who once was a bachelor of story fame.

Last of all is **Lusty**, charming and happy,
She snagged **Tottle** to be her babes new Pappy.
So, Santa's new herd will be on its way,
To deliver the promised on Christmas Day!

The Red Bottle

Every morning as I sit at my computer I look out the patio door facing east. The picturesque view of the hills and mountains is interrupted by a lamp stand on which a red bottle is attached.

The red bottle hangs ever so gentle as it awaits its first morning arrival of the flighty little humming birds.

Sometimes the bottle sways back and forth as the winds dance around the shapely bottle with red tubular feeders and thin red perches.

As always the hungry hummers deplete the nectar from the bottle and in a few days the bottles itself becomes thirsty, craving more nectar.

So once again its master fills its shapely belly to the to the top of its neck .

And low and behold the next day the tiny acrobatic humming birds reward the ever so gentle bottle by filling their precious little bellies too.

Dancing Fingers

Fingers are extensions of my mind that do the bidding of thoughts. They are like little people who pair up for their dances. Ten will equal five, that is, five couples that will please you as they perform dances of all kinds of rhythms and movements.

I visit them every day on my piano to watch their twirling gymnastics as they truly make music and dance upon the keys.

Whether it be tap dance, tango, polka and of course their true love, classical ballet on those black and white keys.

March Winds "A Howlin & A'kicking!"

Winds are sure a'stirring & a'kicking up a
lot of dust around this country's neighborhood.
And believe you me, that ain't good.
The birds are a'flyng upside down
As the wind ruffles their feathery down.
Their feathers are taking a ruffled licking
And the hooting tree owl says, "that ain't good."
Papers a'stirring in the wind, tin cans a'hoppin
Clothes on the line are sure dancing and a floppin.
Hey, there's a man chasing his garbage can
And he's a'runnin as fast as he can.
Matilda Brown, the town's gossip, is crossin the street
But the wind took the wind out of her seat.
Everybody is in an uproar because the gale
Is as big & strong as a giant gray whale,
Elmer got struck in the head by Mrs. Brown's flying pail.
The bell on the church and school house are a' ringing
And it certainly doesn't sound like people singing,
The kids are all laughing at the people's antics
And we all know that Matilda Brown is really frantic.
Who cares about the wind says the little boys
As they all went home to get their toys
That were handmade with precision care
Made of paper, glue, string and wood.
It's a grand day for our kites to take to the air
And with all this commotion flying is sure good.
Mother Nature Did Her Thing
Ended March With A Great Big Fling!

Earth

"How beautiful the earth, water and sky.
Where birds and clouds roam so high.
The sun beams down with rays so sweet
On mounds of rye, clover and wheat.
The moon at night casts it's glow.
The tides run silent, but swiftly flow.
Life is delicate, and who know's best,
Planet earth, our mother's nest."

Shoot That Bow and Arrow

Pull back that string with all your might,
Hold that arrow good and tight.
Now aim for that target at the center ring,
Now release the arrow, and hear it sing.
The arrow's arc looks just right,
With all it's speed and height.
But a sudden wind come up fast,
And the arrow's path does not last.
Well that's a miss, I'll try again.
I really have to blame the wind.
I knew my aim was good and true,
And that friends I really knew.
Practice, practice, shoot that arrow,
And please don't hit that flying sparrow.
I had fun with arrows & bows.
Hitting targets, highs & lows.
With lots of practice it surely shows,
Someday I'll get better, who knows?

Watch Your Glasses,
Or Better Still, No Where They Are!

Joe forgot he put his eye glasses on the bed.

When he sat on the bed he heard and felt a crunching sound. "Oops, I must have sat on something."

He looked down and saw his glasses, the lens had popped out and the frame was bent.

But the lens and frame did not break, what a relief.

Joe called the optical company and told them what happened.

Shirley, the girl who works there said jokingly,

"Oh, I hear that lots of times, people think their eyes are on their bottom."

I thought that was an amusing phrase so I am sharing it with you. Oh, by the way, the glasses are good as new.

Hawk In The Park!

When Dolores and Joe went to Balboa Park to feed the squirrels Sat., Sept. 20, 2003, they saw a man (Dave) chasing and throwing a bag full of peanuts at the largest hawk we had ever seen.

It was very huge and very beautiful, but its still an aggressive predator. It also has to survive.

With no exaggeration (maybe we were excited) the hawk had a wing span of about 2 to 3 feet and was very aggressive. It was flying very low, about 4 feet above the ground trying to grab a squirrel but with no luck.

"This is the first time we ever saw a hawk so close to people. Well no meal for the hawk that day. It's just as well. We came here to feed squirrels not hawks."

When I Was A Kid

I must have been a beautiful baby way back when.
But I changed my ways with a diaper pin.
Then I decided to grow up like all kids do.
Into my skin that sticks like glue.

"What a cute kid your little boy is."
As the lady friend sipped her soda fizz.
All the attention was made for me,
Made my mom proud as can be.

I was not a kid very long, I got older.
My size & facial features got bolder.
Where did that little kid go to hide,
That was so cute, fit to be tied.

When I was a kid, I had it all.
I was happy, I had a ball.
Time passed very quickly & all is gone,
Reminding me at each passing dawn.

My kiddie days went kaput.
Now no one gives a hoot.
We don't stay kids very long
And I think that's awful wrong.

I must have been a beautiful baby.
And if I grow handsome someday maybe.
I'll look into a mirror as I comb my hair
And say to myself, "Smile" if you dare."

My New Year's Resolutions

Making new resolutions for New Years is not easy, especially when your bad habits existed all year long.

When I was a kid, going to school, my teacher said to the class, "It's time to make your New Year's Resolutions."

I really didn't know what that meant. Maybe the other kids knew, but I didn't. I thought that resolutions meant solutions meaning water. So I drank more water and getting water logged was no laughing matter, always running to the bathroom.

Well I finally looked up "resolutions in the dictionary and found a bunch of gobble-de-gook words.

Trying to figure out what those fancy words meant was a real big problem for me.

But the last line really helped me a lot. It said, "Resolve, something that is resolved.

An official determination or simply, "A Formal Resolution. Well anyway......!

After all that studying and to get where I am going, I finally came up with these **10** simple resolutions that I'm going to try to faithfully keep in the new year of 1936, I was 8 years t that time... *Amen.*

1: For my first resolution, I will try to chew my foods longer before swallowing to help ease my constitution.

2: Secondly, I will try to get more sleep and relax my mind more so I can keep out of an institution.

3: Thirdly, I will try to drink at least 8 glasses of solution a day and that makes a great resolution for my constitution.

4: I will watch what I eat. So I sit and watch.

5: I will not watch so much Television. But I can listen.

6: I will exercise more. Take long walks in my sleep.

7: I will not blankity - blank (#@%*&/.!) swear so much.

8: I will spend less time at the computer. Yeah, sure.

9: I will just be a nice person, more friendly and smile more.

10: I will read more classical music compositions and try to commit them to memory.

Well, that's my resolutions, what's yours?

Our Statue of Liberty,
Who Once Saluted
The Mighty Twins of New York City,
Now Weeps With Sadness and Bitterness.

Our Statue of Liberty once saluted the Mighty Twins of
New York City and now she weeps with sorrowed tears and
bitterness for they have disappeared forever.

After the two jets slammed into them and they fell to the
ground, this is what she has to say.

"Yes, my Two Giants who have graced the city's skyline
and created work for our population and once was the
financial capitol of the world are no longer there to serve the
people of this great nation."

America and 60 Nations in all
Will survive after this great fall.

"Yes my children of all races and creed we will come
together and defeat the fears and terror that has come to
terrorize America and the world."

"We will come together, pray, hold hands and succeed in
our rebuilding." All the nations will come together to eradicate
this vermin that has been instilled in our country."

Her torch now pays tribute with each rising dawn
to the Mighty Twins that once were and now gone.
In our our hearts and minds they will always stand
tall in this land, so majestically and so forever Grand.

The Lonely Oak Tree and How Its Life Changed

It all started with a great tall lonely Oak tree
Swaying in the wind, standing there all alone.

"Oh how I wish I could have someone talk to me."
His leaves were crackling and his limbs would moan.

Far across the stretch of land, forests he would see,
Many families of leaves, timber and bark.

He knew they were happy as can be.
But the day is ending and its getting dark.

The winter is cold, there is no on around,
So I'll tuck in my limbs and I'll go to sleep.

The snow is heavy as it falls to the ground
With much silence and is getting deep.

I slept through winter with nights so cold
"I'm still lonely and I'm getting old."

"How can I survive this lonely life,
Without a family and a wife."

Spring is here, and the waters flow,
Feeding all the roots below.

Summer comes with a glowing storm,
Lighting sparkles in all kinds of form.

continues on next page

The Lonely Oak Tree and How Its Life Changed

"What are those little round things in the air?"
"The wind puts them at my trunk as if to dare."

"It plants them in such a natural way,
Am I to coddle them, what can I say."

As time goes by a little seedling grows,
Almost as tall as me, as if it knows.

Nature is set in her way to shoo away my sadness
This is her way to bring me joy and gladness.

At last a wife to bear our seedlings into trees,
There is much to talk about the bird & the bees.

As gentle winds swirl around our leaves & branches,
The acorns & seedlings perform their dances.

The loneliness has gone now,
And to mother nature we bow.

"She has given us the chance to grow
Our trees into forests for all to know."

Now in the night as the moonlight beams,
We talk about our seedlings & their dreams.

They too, someday will stand in our place.
Growing tall & strong at a steady pace.

My Toe and The Rock

As I was playing in the tall grass,
Skipping and hopping and having a blast,
I stubbed my toe on a rock below.
It hurt so bad, it made me mad.

With a tear in my eye, I let out a sigh.
I thought I would surely die.
So off came my shoe and then my sock
To look at my toe that was struck by the rock.

Its starting to swell as it turns black and blue,
Now what am I going to do.
So like a fool I kicked that damn thing
and it paid me back with a much greater sting.

Crawling towards the house on hands and knee,
Don't you know I got stung by a bee
On the very same toe, oh what a blow
To my ego and to my great big toe.

But little did I know when I kicked that rock,
I was going to be in a financial hock.
It struck a window and shattered the glass,
And Mom came out and whipped my ass.

No allowance this month and I'm knowing
That our grass is only good for mowing.
Well there goes one resolution, not to be mad.
Just because its the worst day I ever had.
...So Far!...

Remembering "Valentines Day"
In My Early Grades

Valentine cards were exchanged in my early school years. It was time to give that cute little girl of my thoughts and dreams a Valentine Card to just show her how I felt....You know that,....Puppy Love??

The teacher said not to spend more than a dime. Today it could be a bundle.

I don't remember any gift giving tho, just Valentines were to be given only.

In return I would get a few Valentines from some of my girl admirers.

As I got older Valentines Day kind of drifted away.

Then I met my future wife, Dolores, a blue eyed red headed beauty, she was a beautician. The red hair was dyed, it looked nice. It was around Valentines Day when I was introduced to her. She had on a crimson red suit of Spanish design with lots of buttons in front. Yep, I fell in love. Soooo, I designed and gave her a hugh Valentine Card.

Being that I worked as a typesetter for a Utica, New York newspaper, I made her a hand made Valentine from my printing skills. It was of a double page newspaper size. It was quite large with a headline, subtitles and all, lots of hearts.

Each anniversary I would give her a rose. First year I gave her 1 rose, 2nd year 2 roses. This went on for several years until the tradition wore off. You know we been married for 59 years now and that could contribute a big bunch of roses.

Our loving kids took over the flower giving on Valentines Day with all kinds of different beautiful arrangements that boggle the mind. Happy Valentines Day, Dolores.

Leap Year

To me Leap year means just that..., leaping from here to there.
Some do it just to please others & there are just those who dare.
People who move from one house to another are called leapers.
Some I knew have moved at least 22 times, Jeepers Creepers.
Frogs & Lizards really don't care about the meaning of Leap Year
They leap more than 366 times a day without fear.
Now, let us not forget the leap-second,
Which was devised in 1971, I reckon,
To keep in harmony with solar time.
And does not cost us a nickel or a dime
It compensates for the slowing of the earth rotation,
And that my friends is quite a notation.

The Gregorian solar Calendar contains 365 days in a year and
366 in a leap year; the average is 365 & 1/4. Attempts to establish a
better leap-year rule than the Gregorian are of little value because of
uncertain changes in the Earth's speed of rotation.

So my deduction is:
There are 365 & 1/4 days in a leap year
As the earth rotates without stripping a gear.

The number of days in a year in a religious calendar may vary
widely. The Jewish lunar - solar calendar has from 353 to 355 in a
year and . . . . 383 to 385 in a leap year
in a 19-year cycle. The Moslem lunar calendar, which does not
have leap years, has either 354 or 355 days in a year.
About 33 1/2 Moslem years equal 32 1/2 Gregorian years.

Sooooooo,....my question is,
As I drink my gin fizz,
Saying this with a shout,
What in tarnation are we talking about?

Just ask the frogs & the leaping lizards
To see if this jargon sticks in their gizzards.

Happy Birthday

It's a pleasure to wish
You a Happy Birthday,
What else can one say,

They pile up so fast'
So Have lots of Fun
And make this one last.

Because Next year,
Right around the corner,
Soon, there will be
Another one!

You can't hide,
You can't run,
But you will
Have lots of Fun !!

Sammy,
The Lookout Cat

I am a Cat,
And you know that,
I don't Sit, I Sat.
I'm on the Lookout
For things About,
And when I catch it,
Boy,... do I Shout!

It could be bugs,
It could be plastic,
It could be string.
It I catch it,
I'll Surely Sing.

MEOWWW, MEOWWWWW !!
WOWWWWW, WOWWWWWW !!

Loving You

Loving You Is easy to do.
Especially when it's You!
Loving You With all my heart,
I was struck by Cupids' dart!
Loving You throughout my Life,
For 59 years, you've been my Wife.
Loving you from the guy you know,
From your loving hubby a guy name Joe.

Congratulations To A Graduate
Our Daughter Linda
June 16, 1999

To you Linda, this is what we say,
Here's a cake for you on this happy day.
Now it's over, and you will venture
To a great big wide world adventure.
We love you for what you are.
We are proud of you and you will go far.
So congratulations, hold your head up high
To attain your goal, reach for the sky.
Good Luck,
Lots of Love,
Mom & Dad

Presidents' Day (Poem)

Up, up and away for presidents' day,
And this is what we say,
We had quite a few of them,
But none mention in our anthem.

Oh, say can you see,
In this land of the free.
Oh yes, there will be many more,
Soon there will be forty-four.

The third Monday is set aside to celebrate,
Washington and Lincoln who were great.
Government workers have their days off too
In this land of the red, white and blue.

February has 2 school-free days
So kids can enjoy the sunshine rays.
And let us not forget Valentines Day
In people's heart so they can say.

We send our love to one another
To our family, sister and brother,
To share our freedom in this great land.
That we can walk together hand in hand.

Freedom is a wonderful way
To celebrate Presidents Day
And to express our points and views
Under the flag of reds, whites and blues.

Synonyms
"Words that sound the same but have different meaning"
Tee/Tea: Team/Teem: Saw/Saw: Gear/Gear: Ham/Ham:
Role/Roll: About/About: Drill/Drill: Bit/Bit: Hole/Whole: Hair/Hare:
Fowl/Foul: Game/Game Road/Rode: Be/Bee:

The Pot Hole

As I was crossing the street, I fell into a large deep pot hole.
When I stood up I was able to take in the whole scene.

Looking and staring at me was a great giant white hare.

He was laughing at me because of the mud in my hair.

And to make matters a whole lot worse he started cursing
at me with such foul language.

The chicken across the street didn't mind the the foul
language because he a fowl himself.

Now upon hearing all this cursing, a hunter wanted to play
this game also.

The great white hare with the snowy white hair and the awful
fowl with the foul language was indeed a game delight for the
hunter.

Taking aim at the game, this was now his game. He pulled
the trigger and with a flash, the pellets hurled across the the
road and toward the target they all rode.

"We don't want to play this game game anymore said the
scared white hare with the snowy white hair and and the fowl
with the foul smelling mouth.

Off went the hunter packing his gear rode off on a bicycle
pedalling the gear.

I'll duck back in the hole with a cute little duck, I think its a
safe place to be, Oops, I guess not, I just got stung by great
big Bee.

The moral of this story is when crossing the street,
watch your feet, because that next pot hole you fall in may
10 feet deep.

The Easter Egg
& Its Miracle

Hunting for Easter eggs is lots of fun
As the children look here and there.
Colored bright and hidden under the sun.
When one is found how children stare.
Filling their baskets with eggs to the top,
After days end, home they will go.
As they count them with a skip and a hop.
And trying to put them all in a row.
But wait, an Easter rabbit is hopping behind,
Carrying a secret on this Easter day.
For one of the eggs is showing a sign,
With cracks in the shell and its giving way.
A new life is entering this world of theirs,
To witness this miracle on Easter Day.
The children are in awe with fixed stares.
They are silent, what can they say.
This egg was not to be foiled
And that was meant to be
Thank goodness it was not hard boiled
For inside was a live chick-a-dee

First Day of Spring

If you see a robin pulling up a worm
It could be a sign of an early Spring,
If the worm he is pulling doesn't squirm
The robin may not try to sing.
To see a running stream, it may be an early Spring
If the stream gets all iced up and stops its flow
Fish and toads and cool water it can not bring
To those waiting to see Mother nature's show.

"Good Friday"

The Friday before Easter is set aside as
the anniversary of the crucifixion of Christ.
In some states it as a legal holiday.

My Poem Is This:
My first encounter with "Good Friday"

When I was young and silent in tongue,
In my ear I heard a rung.
"Children should seen and not heard."

We could not fly and sing like a bird,
We only believed in stories that we heard.

Robinson Caruso was a shipwrecked fellow,
Alone on and island, oh how he would bellow,

The loneliness he could not bear
He wanted his life to share.

He fell to his knees upon the hot sand
And prayed to God and raising a hand.

"I would like to have a friend I could talk to
Work with me, laugh with me and not feel blue.

His prayers were answered when a native appeared,
He looked at me, I looked at him, it was so weird

I taught him to read and all what I knew,
I gave him a name which I will later tell you.

He was so good to me and helped all he would,
He would smile and I know he understood.

We were alone together on this island of no where.
We got along together and ideas we would share.

Oh, To Be Irish

Oh, to be Irish is indeed a way of life,
Happy as can be with a pretty wife.
She'll have red hair and eyes of green,
A very pretty lass you've ever seen.

Then we'll have children,
They'll be chips of the ole' block,
Their talents will be musical
That will make you surely rock.

We'll soar through this great Emerald Land,
Which is known as our home, Ireland.
Our children will lead the marching band,
In this land which is ever so grand.

Their music may be an Irish Jig or a nice sounding Reel,
Dancing to them, their beats and rhythms you will feel.
Ireland's music is known the world over,
Just like its great fields of flowers and clover.

The Irish Pub awaits its' visits from the locals around,
So they can guzzle their drinks, round after round.
They fill their stomachs with a delicious Irish Sub,
Made from the local neighborhood's, "Ye Ole Pub."

Now what about that tin pail of green ale,
From the Pub we sent our 'Junior' to get,
And hoping he'll not turn green with an Irish fit,
Sometimes his Irish temper gets riled up just a bit.

Now going back home, in the fields he'll pick a flower,
Taking it to his mom after a nature's brief shower.
It could be a "Shamrock" or a "Four Leaf Clover."
For all of his family to enjoy its scent over and over.

Oh, to be Irish is such a grand way to be,
Surrounded by that beautiful giant emerald sea.
The scenic views are beautiful to behold,
And its mythical stories will forever be told.

Kissing that "Blarney Stone" or catching an elf,
Or following that rainbow in the sky of blue,
Making wishes for your family and yourself.
How happy everyone will be if they all come true.

Superstition?

If one is ignorant of a fact & one practices a belief in witch does
not exist, than superstition becomes evident.
This opinion may seem harsh to those who believe in
magical folklore handed down generations to generations.
Some examples of this are:
Indian Folklore, Black Magic, Witchcraft, Greek Mythology and others
that may involve the supernatural like Ghosts, Possessiveness or
Possessed by Demons and Magical Beings,
Irish Elves (Leprechauns) and perhaps the greatest of them all:

HALLOWEEN is when kids & adults dress in their costumes.
Also called All Hallows' Eve holiday, Oct. 31, now observed largely as
a secular celebration. It is practiced all over the world. As the eve of All
Saints' Day, it is a religious holiday among some Christians.

A Superstition Poem, Its Practices & Beliefs

If one were to practice the so called Black Magic
Its impossibility could very well prove to be tragic
Thinking that we can pull our lives, like rabbits out of the Hat
To make our lives more financial as if to get fat.
Superstition Mountain contains a lode of gold
Dug up by the Dutchman who was so bold.
High up in the mountains, it still remains there.
Try finding it if you dare, its like pulling your hair.

Friday 13th, the unlucky day, don't walk under that ladder or you will pay.
Breaking that mirror into tiny bits, could drive you out of your friggin wits.
If a Black Cat cuts in front of you, don't cross its path or you may get blue.
Bad luck comes in all shapes & forms, try to weather its mighty storms.
Don't point your finger at the North Star or you'll surely get warts.
Don't take short cuts through a cemetery, bad luck will come in all sorts.
But no matter what we think of superstition, we all like to play its game.
Its fantasies and make believe, the stories all come out the same.
These mythical stories of superstition will continue in our world,
So in your minds, make believe, play its game and give it a whirl.

Lost In A Dream

Some times I'm lost in a dream.
There's no light, no life, what does it mean.
The stillness and emptiness makes me wonder,
There's no weather here, no sound of thunder.
No glimmer of moonbeams, no sun showers.
No trees, no grass, no brooks, no flowers.
No stars that twinkle, no sparkles that gleam.
Am I trapped here forever, what does it mean.

There's no wind on my face, I don't feel a thing.
No music here, cannot even sing.
I can not hear my voice, I can not talk,
I can not see a path on which to walk.
If I don't wake up, what does this mean.
I cannot cry, should I redeem.
All my sins of the past,
Or must I stay here, steady and fast.

Am I to stay forever in this blackened hell,
I can not scream or even yell.
But wait, something is going on in my ear,
There is a clamor of sound, I can hear.
I was scared with the worst of fears.
But the morning sounds delighted my ears
I felt I was bound by a strangling rope,
I struggled to move. Is there still hope?

So I slapped my face as hard as I could,
My body and mind understood.
I quickly arose from out of my bed,
Was it the closest to being dead.
My dreams are getting better,
So I'll write them down in this letter,
I'm still trying to get it all together,
With sweet smells from flowers and heather.

My dreams are now full of spice,
With colorful skies and fields of rice.
People will marry as church bells ring
Happiness is here, now I can sing.

Baseball

Take me out to the Ball Game,
All nine players, you can name,
Buy them some peanuts and crackerjack,
Let's see now, if they can comeback.

Three bags and a plate,
Brother, that's their fate.
One bat, one ball, its us for all
Playing the diamond like a musical dance hall.

For its one, two, three and he's out,
Saying what's this game all about
Heres' to the winners who beat us bad.
Its the worse game we ever had.

Peanuts, popcorn, get em' here,
Have a can of that cold foamy beer.
Get your hot dogs while there hot,
All this food will hit the spot.

And buy the kid a candy bar
Named after "Babe Ruth"
He hit that ball so dang far,
The out fielder couldn't see it,
...And it broke his tooth.

Lets play ball cries the umpire to the batter in the box,
Then the pitcher hurls the ball, he's sly as a fox.
Swoosh! As he swings, "that's a strike", Umpire shouts.
And the batter just stands, amazed and pouts.

Then Fox throws a curve ball that is struck with such force,
Out of the ball park it goes hitting a cop on a horse.
A home run for sure from our home town boy.
And the standing crowd roars and shouts with joy.

BASEBALL...continues on next page

Baseball

But the cop on the horse got a lump on his head.
And batter is glad because he wasn't dead.
So he sign the ball and gave it back to the cop.
Along with candy, hot dog and a sodie pop.

The next batter is up, and the sly Fox throws,
The crowd Boos from way high in the back rows
Strike one, strike two and strike three.
Your out, shouts the umpire, out as can be.

Craziest ball I've ever seen,
Like hitting a pitch from Dizzy Dean.
But the score on the board goes up and down.
And out comes the coach with a great big frown.

Give me that ball, your outta hear.
The Foxy pitcher walks off with fear.
What the blankity, blank does he want from me.
I played my best game for all to see.

Well we lost that game and the crowd goes home
Drinking their beer thats now warm with foam.
Our home town team didn't do too good.
Maybe they need bats with harder wood.

So a hardwood tree was chopped down for the team.
And new bats were milled from the electrical machine.
Yes, the harder bats brought luck to the home town team,
Now winning all of the games, their right on the beam.

The tree was struck by lightning, that gave them a charge.
The bats were of official size, not small or not large.
But they had a kick that like a swift Arabian horse
Just like that cop who was hit, now in remorse.

Good luck team, Yea!   March 17, 2008

Strange Odd People

If you're a stranger in this town,
You may be tagged as a curious clown.
You may be an odd ball to some
Or just like the hobo who is a bum.

Being a genius, smart and odd,
You could be a great golfer on the sod.
A hole in one is what we aim for,
But under par would be a great score.

Einstein was odd, with a hefty brain,
But didn't know enough to come out of the rain.
He calculated formulas with out much pain
And became so odd, we thought him insane.

Vincent Van Gogh was odd and insane,
He cut off his ear and yelled with pain.
Robert Schumann tried stretching his hands.
He was an odd one, but his music still stands.

Strange as it seems, how odd one can be,
Like Nostradamus, the future he could see.
Richard Wagner wrote operas for us to hear,
Forced us to listen & did cartwheels as we sat in fear.

Now to all the odd people on this globe,
Don't pull out your hair and don't disrobe.
Try to keep your wits about you.
We know your odd, don't feel blue.

Diet

A nibble here and a nibble there
And a nibble on that sweet juicy pear
If I eat my greens and lots of fruit
I won't be such a big fat brute.

But I still think of all that pasta I used to eat.
I got so heavy, couldn't stand on my feet.
Well that's over now, my diet is working fine.
I'm getting skinny and so is my behind.

Now I'm walking tall, with my head up high,
Knowing that I can have that piece of pie.
Seen my doctor and he said with a sigh,
"If you didn't diet, you would surely die.

Toys

A Toy is something that makes you happy,
Given to you by your mammy or pappy.
It could be a sled, skates or a checker set,
A 'BB'gun, a bike or a cute furry pet.

When I was a little boy,
I had a special toy.
Up and down it would go,
It was my little Yo-Yo.

It was made in a Northern Factory,
Approved and stamped satisfactory.
A little Elf made it with "Blinking Lights,"
That danced & glowed in the darkened nights.

Sometimes Toys are made here at home
By the Toy Maker with beard &a shiny dome.
See him in the window on any given day,
Making toys for children so they can play.

The Bells Toll Ominously

It was a dark, dark night, hardly a star was out, no fireflies,
no moon, just pitch black.

The air was still and close, no wind, no movement.
No one was around, everyone was gone.
They were not sleeping, not even breathing.

The people were still, no life, no sound. No locals to be seen
or heard in the town.

Just then from the sky a clap of rolling thunder shook the
ground and all that was under.

And suddenly the bells in the chapel, on the rolling grounds
dotted by grayish whitish stones, began to toll ominously as
if struck by the devil himself.

Was it an omen of evil or just a mighty hand pealing the
bells for the entrance of another soul to be grounded under
the yonder knoll.

As the story is told by the folks of the town, it was just
another way of saying hello to the newly arrived visitors.

For they all knew that the Bells in the Chapel will and always
toll Ominously.

RATS

What has 4 legs, a short body with a long a tail, long whiskers, black
beady eyes, warts on its' nose and head, black or brown matted hair
with big gnawing teeth that eats wood just like our friendly termites and
leaves black or brown stinking droppings all over our dwellings because
he likes to eat stinking cheese?. . . .

Why it's the SEE THAT AWFUL RAT of Our Story
STAR is RATS backwards

Rats, Rats, Rats, the're all over you see.
They came here by boats from across the sea.
Their population is excessively high,
Just like bugs, mosquitos and the fly.

The husky mooring ropes for the large boats
Became highways for our dirty furry flea bitten hosts.
The round metal shields on the ropes didn't work very well,
The Rats merely climbed over them to bring us Holy Hell.
They ravaged our homes and live in the dumps
And will sicken you with disease or even the mumps.
Their filthy bodies, infested by germs
Brings plight, strong odors and even worms.
But still many of us have a pet thats a rat,
It could be brown, white, skinny or fat.
Not fully aware that our pet is just that,
And the game that they play is 'Tit for Tat'.
To clean the ugly filth from its cage
Puts us in an awful rage.
If we don't clean it very well
Their droppings will present an awful smell.
So let's think hard about the year of the rat,
In some countries they eat them just to get fat.
But all in all they are still ugly animals.
If we don't watch out, they may become our cannibals.

April Fool Joke

Hey Honey! . . ."Hurry up and get out of bed,
The house is on fire,". . . hear what I said ?
She got up sleepily and looked around,
There's no fire here, not even a sound.

Then he laughed and jokingly said,
"Ha, Ha, Ha, . . . APRIL FOOL ! . . . his face was all red.
Now fuming and mad, worse morning she ever had.
That's mean and that wasn't funny honey. that was bad.

"But wait, hold still," she said, still in a rut.
There's a Giant Green Bug on your butt.
And saying that, she kicked him hard in the rear.
And He yelled so loud, it hurt her ear.

He pulled his pants down to see the Giant Green Bug.
Why there's nothing here, not even on the rug.
"Ha, Ha, Ha, . . . APRIL FOOL ! . . . You great big Lug.
And with that, they made up with a Giant Big Hug.

Winkle and Matilda's April Fool

Hello Mrs. Winkle, please come in, have a chair
As she sat down they started to chat.
I'm trying to thin down to get rid of my fat.
"Oops, Matilda said, I forgot, I just painted that.
Winkle quickly got up with an awful mean stare.
I just bought this dress along with my new hat
Now their ruined as she pulled out her hair.
Awww, April Fool, you'll be okay.
Oh Yeah, but you ruin my day.
And I think you should pay.
Matilda felt bad, didn't know what to say.
Yeah, I pulled out my hair and now my hats' too big.
Winkle looked at Matilda, paused for a moment, and said.
April Fool to you Matilda it was only a wig.

Weather, Showers and Tornado

There is a eerie chill in the air,
The wind is pushing its way.
Animals are running to their lair,
They know its going to be a bad, bad day.

Its not a mild shower,
Thats coming to strike the earth,
It looks like a curved black cloud,
With lightning and thunder, extremely loud.

It knifes through a farm land
And levels a red barn to the ground.
Nature has unleashed her mighty power,
A tornado is born with shrieking sound.

Blackened skies are filled with knives,
There's danger everywhere.
Run to your shelters, save your lives,
Do not face this menace if you dare.

Wood from the red barn can be used for fire.
The storm was costly, we lost our crop.
Money is scarce, we cannot hire.
The well is destroyed, and nary a drop.

This evil has gone now and left its mark,
Soon the skies opened with a gentle plan.
Soft fluffy white clouds replaced the dark
With cool dancing showers upon the land.

Unfortunately,
Things Fell Apart Almost Immediately

Upon getting up in the morning, I remembered that I had to go to the bank to conduct some business transactions.

I was to get some cash and make some money transfers.

Sooo..., I put my Visa Card in the mouth of the ATM machine and entered my pin number as requested by the screen's monitor.

But the ATM machine quickly spit it out and on the screen appeared "Sorry Wrong Number."

Sooo..., I entered the pin number again and to my surprise, again..."Sorry Wrong Number."

Sooo..., I entered the pin number again and to my surprise, again..."Sorry Wrong Number."

I must have punched in the wrong 4-digit pass number.

But this time the ATM machine in all its glory, "Ate" my Visa card.

"Then,..unfortunately things fell apart almost immediately."

The bank was about to close and there just a couple of floor representatives helping other people. I waited and waited and then I was told to come back after the long weekend.

They heard my story but to no avail. What am I to do.

Can't make a check out for the rent, no extra cash in my pockets to spend.

I felt like I was in a deep, deep void.

I fell completely apart. But, after a while things did finally get straighten out.

Now its your to turn to tell your 'Falling Apart Story.'

Memorial Day, May 30th

When I was very young and growing up, my parents took me to the local graveyard. It was my first visit and a very good learning experience for me.

It is and still now centrally located on Mohawk Street in Utica, New York. And there is a florist, conveniently located across the street of the cemetery. How well I remember that.

It was a pleasant day, the sun was shining bright and there were gentle winds and very quiet.

Entering the cemetery, we walked the paths as my parents pointed out the stones and monuments where most of the Soldanos are buried.

I didn't say too much while we were walking. I just looked around at all the flowers that were placed on the grounds.

Some monuments were very hugh and some were very small.
It didn't matter what size they were because the flowers seemed to match the dignity of the grave.

There was an eerie feeling about the graves, especially the one with statues of Angels and baby angels.

My parents put some flowers on my relatives grave sites and said prayers and then we left.

It wasn't too long after that when my cousin Salvatore was killed in WWII (World War 2). My Aunt Angie and Uncle Dick got the bad news that he was killed on Christmas Eve. He was a rear gunner on an airplane bomber B19 or B51. He was shot down over Germany.

They had to wait for the warmer weather to bury my cousin. It was, I believe, on Memorial Day.

All the family was there, there a lot of people that I didn't even know. It was a military funeral. Soldiers all dressed up in their colors. The American flag waving. The priest gave an eulogy and the Sargent of Arms saluted and gave a command.

Then there was a gun salute that was very loud and all the people started to cry. I will never forget that day. That is what memorial day means to me. Every year I relive that day and say a prayer.

It Ain't Like That No More

The lowest gasoline prices I recall was 14 to 16 cents a gallon. Gasoline prices were affordable then, but today forget it. Eggs and bread were to be had for a mere pocket change. Today they are in the dollar bracket. Years ago a couple bags of groceries could be had for around 5 bucks. Well today "It ain't like that no more."

Things were a lot cheaper in my days. Movies, 10c to a quarter. Ice cream cones, a nickel, 7 to 12 caramels were a penny. Caramel Corn was another cheap item, 25c a bag. "It ain't like that no more."

I remember some of these prices because there was a store named "Troussets", just kitty corner from my house. My late cousin Rocky Soldano used worked there. When I had a penny I could get my moneys worth than.

There was a cherry tree just in front of the store and I would pick some of the cherries, they were free. How many cherry trees do you see for the pickins around the neighborhood. "It ain't like that no more."

Yep, "Times have changed" and "It Ain't Like That No More, It sure Ain't."

Watches, Clocks, Chimes,
Gongs and Sun Dial

My obedient friend is there when I need it,
Its smiley face shows me its' dial when lit.
The hands circles the face as if to speak,
It serves me the time with each passing week.
Majestic is their way, quietly ticking the passing of the sublime.
Whether it would be a watch, clock, gong, sun dial or chime.
Listen to the gong as it hums its eerie resonated song.
Or the ticking of the clock leading its mighty flock.
The heart of life pulses its merry tune like a watch on a wrist.
Keeping time for us to exist as we sway our body with a clinching fist.
We move in time, we exist in time, we live in time.
Hey buddy!...Do you know the time of day?
A common question needlessly to say.
Yes, of course its free to everyone.
Mornings, noon, nights and when the day is done.
Our life in a day, is governed by its main spring.
Just like the valued notes of a song we might sing.
Our inner clock is running with a steady beat
Life goes on and that my friends is quite a feat.

Ghosts

The night comes with all its presence and stirring of the flukes,
The 31st of October is here and gives way to the howling Spooks.
Or it may any day to pick on people just to spook,
We'll get them so nervous, they'll bend over sick and puke.
The ghosts of war with its flying spooks
We'll not forget the war of the atomic nukes
An Asian city wiped out with a mighty blast
Now lives with a horrifying past.
The Poltergeist is a nagging creation of the devil full of sins
Living in the bowels of the earth in blackened coal bins
Sending the ghost that manifests itself by noises that ring in your ear,
His creation of disorder, rapping on doors to cause you fear.

When I Found Out I Wasn't Immortal

Upon reading about famous people who have survived the ages of time and became immortal and legends of their own, I finally decided that I was not immortal. I was destined to pass away and soon be forgotten on this earth.

When I was a young boy, I would wake up in the mornings and felt like I would live forever. Death never occurred to me, so I just lived my youthful days to the fullest capturing as much joy and happiness that would pass my way.

I would visit my relatives, Grandparents, Aunts and Uncles. As time passed and my Grandparents were no longer with me, I realized that I too was getting on in the years. Then my Uncles, Aunts , my parents and even my cousins who were my age left to another world.

When I came here to California 30 years ago, time passed so fast I completely forgotten my friends in my home town. I decided to look them up, give them a call on the phone and to my surprise, I found that most of them have gone to the other side.

Fortunately I have only one close friend who I communicate with. There are a few others that I know and send my Newsletters. They are the only ones left.

Now I realize that finding out that I too wasn't Immortal, I will leave that position up to the Gods, the Legends of famous writers, painters, inventors and so on and so on. Its nice to read all about their famous gifts to mankind through history.

Yes, I am only a mere mortal who probably will pass through these portals of existence and just fade away when the time comes of my demise with no immortality to my name, who knows?.

Every Family Has Their Own Immortality

I'll walk this path just once in my life.
Arm in arm with Dolores, my beautiful wife.
Who has shared and gave birth,
To our children, their families on this earth.
That may be Immortality, in itself, that we try to proclaim.
Each and every family in their own right has their own fame.

Tiny Grains of Sand

Try counting the grains in a cup of sand
And marking the time that was on hand.
Counting each grain again, again & again.
Now that time whatever if may have been.

How long did it take to count those grains?
Doing this it will numb you brains.
Your back will ache and you'll be in pain.
After all that counting, what did you really gain.

Multiply it by all the time it takes
Whether it would be a day or week for goodness sakes.
Then start over with a another cup of sand
As you count each grain with a trembling hand.

Your eyes will squint with moist salted tears
Try not to sneeze or it will be your worst fears.
If you do the wind blown grains will sail away
Making it impossible to count the grains another day.

Music

Music, music is my game
As I tag them with my humble name.
Some are happy, some are sad
If you pick the right one, you'll be glad.

My life is music as it was for my kin.
We all composed songs that's never been.
Music came out of the air & into our ears.
If the song was sad it brought you to tears.

How easy it is to write down a note,
It may be the easiest thing you've ever wrote
The staff has 5 lines & 4 spaces
If you get an idea then your off to the races.

Do, re, me are the notes as I hum this tune,
I'll get it done & pretty soon.
Now take the piano that I like to play
My composition I'll play for you if I may.

We're Getting Old

First let me say, "This poem is not intended for the ill."
With uncontrollable sickness, and are losing their will.
We must honor and cherish them, they are part of our life.
They have their way of coping with personal strife.

The biggest complaint we get from our peers
And probably the the most of our hidden fears,
Is the fact that "We're getting old" and if I may be bold
I must say, it's the same old story ever told.

Did we forget the days when we were small
And looked up to the folks that were older and tall.
Our childhood is written from beginning to end,
With memories in our hearts that will never bend.

In our journey we all have ripened with age,
With humor, pain, sickness and sometimes with rage.
Ah, to be young again is beyond our soul,
Only to dig deeper into the bottomless hole.

Is our dignity still with us, or do we just hang in there?
With many blows to our chin, is life so hard to bear?
Life has been good to all us as we continue our ride.
Many of our birthdays were celebrated with awesome pride.

We may complain, make excuses, but we still journey on.
Our hair turns to gray that was once red, brunette or blonde.
We go to the movies, watch TV, socials, or even date
Enjoy talking to friends, life is nice, what's there to hate?

Mom used to say, "why don't you grow up."
Your always whining just like a young pup.
When you get there, you'll see what I mean.
You'll be just like an old oiled machine.

So next time you hear that same old song, "We're getting old."
Just listen and learn from those who are gilded in gold.
They have succeeded in taking life and ringing its the neck.
So we must say, "We're getting Old, so what the heck."

What If I Did Change Course?

    If I had to do it all over again I guess I would have done a lot of things differently.

    I would have paid more attention to my mother's cooking. Especially when she told us what she put in her meals. She was so proud of her cooking. I would have jotted down all her recipes and all the kids would cherish the Golden Menus.

    If only I kept all my toys. They could have been collector items. If I save my first penny/savings. All my pennies, nickels and dimes in the piggy bank. Throughout the years I had many of them. I would need a humongous house/barn to put it all in and thus I would become a modern "KING MIDAS"

My Favorite Thing

My favorite thing was taking my girl out Sunday
To go to the Sweet Shope for our favorite delight.
We would also go there on Saturday & Monday
For our favorite sweet delight, oh what a sight.

Vanilla ice cream drenched in hot soup
Topped off with a cherry of red
And whipped cream decorated loop by loop.
At night I would dream of it when I went to bed.

Hot soup you say? I meant dripping hot fudge.
It was only 15 cents way back when.
We ate so much of it we couldn't budge.
Our friends used to say, "We knew you've been.

My girl & I would say, "Yes, today is Monday."
So off to the Sweet Shope we went for our favorite thing.
Yep, you guessed it was our favorite Hot Fudge sundae.
Its sweetness was so pleasurable it would make us sing.

My First Day With The Bulb

It was a very dark cloudy afternoon when I got out of school. As I was walking home, I noticed there was a dim glimmer of light emitting through the windows from some of the neighboring homes that I usually pass by.

It was a strange and eerie observation. The kids outside appeared nervous and at the same time a little scared of the new addition to their homes. I asked them what was the problem. Excitingly they said, "You'll find out when you get home." "Hmmmn, well I'll just have to wait."

it was dark when I finally got home. I climb up the steps to the second floor where I live. My mother and father were excited and it was very dark in the kitchen.

"Where's all the candles and kerosene lamps?" I asked. "It's dark in here, can't see!"

My mother calmly took my hand and said, "Feel this string, now pull it gently."

With that said, I pulled the string gently, I should say yanked it and to my surprise a bright glow appeared from a little glass pear shaped thing-a-ma-jig.

Very surprisingly I stepped back with my face full of sunshine. Wow that's kind of weird, just like magic!.

What is it? My father said it's a light bulb powered by electricity. We don't have to use the candles or lamps for lighting anymore unless the power goes off.

That was my first day or should I say with the bulb.

I curiously looked at it. The glass was clear. It was a little smaller than an 'eating pear'. Inside was some fine wires that looked like an insect or a praying mantis. Thanks to the inventer, Thomas Alva Edison for modernizing our house.

As long as I could remember we always had running water and now electricity and now the Bulb." That's what I first called it and to this day I call them bulbs.

Continues on next page...

My First Day With The Bulb

Some of the kids on the block would brag about their new electric refrigerator. We still had the old ice box and coal stove. It was a job just to get coal and ice in those days.

I had to lug ice a couple of blocks. Coal I had to get from the cellar and carry it upstairs to the second floor.

One day my father took my mother to the appliance store to see the new electric refrigerators and gas stoves. After he bought them, he threw out the ice box and coal stove.

I really miss the old stove because we used to put orange peels and roast pumpkin seeds on it, what a nice flavored scent it was for the holidays.

With all these new modern inventions popping up, what's in store for us in the future?

Cell phones, I-pods, HD-TVs, computers, computerized cars, etc. etc. What's next?...and with our new fangled refrigerators it's kind of funny that we still go to the store to buy ice cubes for the soda & beer cans for picnics even though our fridges can make ice cubes. Sometimes we still resort to the old ways of doing things.

"An Ode to the Bulb"

The bulb was off, there was no light.
There was no string in sight.
I have to find that string
Or there'll be no light to bring
I finally found it, I'll give it a fling
As I pulled it it made the door bell ring.
Then I found another string, I pulled it,
Behold the "Bulb" glowed so bright, the room was lit.
Yet hanging, there was another string,
I shall not pull it for I don't know what it will bring.
Now today we have it all, I confess,
With all this electronic stuff we have a mess.

14 days . . .
1: 2: 3: 4: 5: 6: 7: 8: 9: 10: 11: 12: 13: 14:

A Poem Line In Two Weeks

Day

1: Because there's 14 days in 2 weeks, I'll write a
line a per day.

2: The second line will rhyme with the first, each day
will follow its way.

3: Thirdly I'm thinking of the things I did, how
important they were.

4: Fourthly I'll round up all the pets in town and pet
their fur.

5: On my fifth day I will will take those pets & find
them a home.

6: On day six I found each one a home so they can
no longer roam.

7: The seventh day seems to be a lucky number for
me, I'll play the Lotto.

8: Day eighth I won a modest sum, so I'll make up a
playful Motto.

9: On day nine my motto is this, "If you don't play the
lotto you can't win."

10: On day ten you'll get the lotto results, you didn't
play, now ain't they a sin

11: Eleventh day is another lucky number when you
roll those spotted dice.

12: Twelfth day everyone listen, don't gamble, says
your parents, take their advice.

13: On the day of the thirteenth, if its Friday, their
advice to you is to stay in.

14: Because on the fourteenth day you'll get your
stimulus check & that's a win.

I Wonder

Did you ever wonder why the sun rises & sets?
Too give day light & darkness as it rests.
I wonder why it rains & why there is snow.
As water makes the forest trees grow & grow.

I wonder what mother nature has in store for us
With all her storms & all the fuss.
She beautifies the land with all her magic
And takes it away with volcanic eruptions, that's tragic.

I wonder why life is lived in vain, what's there to gain
I wonder why we age with sickness & live with pain.
I wonder why earth people grow so very old.
I wonder why God makes us die & breaks the mold.

As I write this, I wonder with amazement
Why some homes have furnaces in the basement.
I often wonder how my feet fit into the Bronze shoes.
I often wonder why some stories make the news.

Well, I can wonder all day long
As I compose & write this song
That my life is mine to keep
As I ride away in my merry old Jeep.

I wonder where the winding roads will take me
Into the country side, a great wondrous land to see.
I wonder if all the people are as happy as me.
And I mostly wonder what's really in store for Thee.

Newly Weds

The wedding was beautiful and performed with grace,
The Bridal gown was trimmed with silk & lace.
The Groom was handsome & said "I do."
His Bride at his side said "Me too." .

The wedding cake has 4 tiers & on its' very top
The statues of the Bride & Groom skipped with a hop.
The cake is well decorated, ah so sugary sweet.
A piece of cake to all, with many guests to greet.

After sharing vows, together they now belong.
The bride & groom dance to their wedding song.
Daddy's little girl is not very small,
And mommies little boy is now very tall.

Rice was thrown like hail from the sky
As the newly weds gave out with a sigh.
We're married now and we belong,
We'll raise a family, it won't be long.

Off went the car with a trail of cans.
Good luck was shouted from from all their fans.
We'll see you all later the newlyweds said.
We're glad you had a nice time& were well fed.

"She Was A Beautiful Cat, Our Little Pearl"

Sammy was 19 years old, she had a long happy life.
Our Siamese with 4 white paws was company for my wife.
She had a loud voice like a soprano opera singer.
With high & low notes that would continue to linger.

We sprinkle Catnip on the floor,
It makes her tipsy & she wants more.
Eating it, she'll give her tail a tug,
As she rolls & flips all over the rug.

Her daily antics were cute as can be
She was always there for you & me.
She'll rub her face on your leg & curl her tail around it
As if to say, "Please pet me just a little bit."

At night, in the middle of the room, she would sit & stare,
As we watched television in a comfortable chair.
Then she would jump onto my wife's lap,
And there she would curl up to take her nap.

Her purrs were so loud as she slumbered away
And please don't wake me or ther'll be hell to pay.
Her tail would quiver and her paws would curl.
She was our pet, so sweet, our little pearl.

Her fondness of memories are still with us today
Having a pet to love, what could one say.
We stroke their fur and wonder as they purr.
Was her life on earth just a passing blur.

Voting

To vote or not to vote, that is the question?

We have been given certain inalienable rights because our forefathers were able to foresee the future. The citizens of America were granted these rights because it would make our democracy much more independent than those living in other countries around the world.

The right to vote in a candidate of your choosing at the voting polls for a selected public office with a check mark, punch the Chad or a click of the switch made for a free society. Or putting your ballot in the box.

Sometimes we wished we had voted for the other guy. Then we would sit around & argue how the candidates, president, governor, mayors & other governmental officials were doing. How much graft was for the taking.

If they promised to lower taxes, they were doing good, they were the good guys, we would brag about them, if not, we would have to wait for the next election to get screwed again.

That much sums up the voting in this country in my opinion.

Swim Suits

Many years ago the swim suit covered the whole body even with a fancy swim hat. One couldn't swim long distances in those days unless that pealed off the heavy garment down to their shorts to make the a very long swim.

In 1855 2 tiered fluke hooped female swim came into existence to cover up the bare skin of a female.

The suit also had a pair of long pantaloons covering up the legs because in those days it was unheard of to show too much skin. Women didn't worry about skin cancer in those days due to the sun's harmful ultra violet rays. Their skin was always pure & white like Ivory..

The men on the other hand had more freedom. Their swim suits had tank tops bearing their arms and slightly long pants bearing their muscular legs. They looked kind of silly with long mustaches & beards in their striped black & white outfits.
I guess men had more freedom in those days.

Now today is a different story, styles have changed

In France, skimpy swimsuits allow women to bear their breast.
But here in America our laws are more rigid than the rest.
We have that dotted Bikini that bears the girlie mass,
And I'm not speaking of the donkey, mule or cute little Jack Ass.
Sometimes in private, a couple will swim in the moon light.
No bathing suits are needed for this wondrous sight.
Our children's parents know best, innocence is theirs to keep.
Later in age if their swimsuits come off, Moms & Pops may weep.

Fireworks

The first fireworks I heard was my father shotgun booming out the window. In those days you could get away with almost anything. He used a shotgun because the small fine bee-bees became harmless way in the air and when they fell no one got hurt. Unlike the rifle bullet that was clump of lead and if that came down a person could probably get killed.

My first fireworks was the sparkler, waving it about in the dark and creating different designs was fun. But boy do that burn if you get some of the hot melting on you.

When we were kids, the dare was putting a very little firecracker between our teeth and setting if off. We really got a bang out of that. that was a little wacky.

Commercialism put the damper on firework displays. Now its done by pyro professionals and in my opinion its not like the old days when you could sit in the public parks and be close to the the firework displays. Just back enough so you were not in danger. The displays would last longer. The best one was the waterfalls and a flaming man would dive into it.

I'm not knocking it per say, but everyone is blowing up their can of worms and their is no surprises to them anymore. They all look the same.

The old firework displays had more imagination, more spark, more fire. The good ole days are gone, just memories.

Every weekend you hear the distant sounds of fireworks from the famous Seaworld. So what's new.

Poetry To Prose

When will the words of rhyme end?
Finding them makes my mind bend.
If I can't find rhymes anymore
I'll write down prose I do implore.

Prose

Writing Prose is much easier for me. Ideas come faster, and puts my mind more at ease just like the tranquillity of the waves that are capped with foam of white above the dark blue sea waters that are clear and sparkling bright like little shimmering delights.

Writing prose is like painting with words, so many colors to choose from from the palate.

A sheet of paper will be my canvas and my pen will be my trusty brush and mind will be the creator.

Casting colors upon the canvas is not to rhyme but to harmonize colorful hues will be my goal.

The hues of palatable colors will make my painting more pleasing to eyes of the beholder.

My picture will speak a thousand words.

As I brush along this canvas with the pleasures of prose painting words of colors, vividly coming to my mind, it becomes for me, a state of rest.

The Mighty Wave

As the mighty wave churns with foam, winds carries its wet coolness to relieve the dryness on my face. The long day's sun is giving way for pleasurable things that is yet to come.

Our eyes are the soul for observing the beauty this earth has given us.

As the day ends and the sun falls deeply in sleep, there is no light to see with if the moon is hiding behind its bed of clouds.

The darkness is now with us but we can still hear the waves as they roil with the tide.

Our mind now creates imaginary visions if there is no light.

Our imagination is only the reflection of the its perpetual sight.

Our Sun

A brief summation of earth's closest star, our faithful furnace for our mother earth.

93 million miles away in the celestial heavens there is a firery molten mass that is our, the earth's, life source for all living things on it. Planets revolve around it as the moon revolves us in their designated orbital highways according to physical laws

It's locked in space for all to see and upon the earth it casts many, many shadows proving our existence.

It contains almost every known element to man but in extremely blistering nuclear form.

It generates its energy by nuclear fusion in its core. The sun is extremely difficult & impossible to get at. Everyone knows its much too hot.

Flying

Ever since time began, man looked toward the sky.
He looked at the flying wonders and said, "Maybe I could fly."
How can I get up there with those creatures of wings?
I do not have wings of feathers, what are those things?

So I netted a wonder and studied this beauty.
It was a humming bird, it was a cutie.
I fashioned some wings out of old chicken feathers.
To fit my torso like a snug feathered sweater.

I flapped my wings, I was flying high.
If I fell to earth, I would surely die.
All went well but the birds made a fuss.
What is this strange creature flying with us?

My arms got tired, so I'll think I'll land.
I hurtled to earth into a mound of sand.
This is my story and I'm not lying.
I was high in the sky, I was really flying.

Hard Luck

The weather was blistering frigidly cold & the ground was hard as stone. Light snow was churning in the area.

Little children were sent & seen in the 40s walking along the railroad tracks picking up pieces of coal dropped off from the coal cars. They gathered as much coal they possibly could but their little fingers were frozen to the bone.

If a child came home with a full bucket of coal, the reward would be a mug of hot chocolate. They would wrap their little hands around the hot mug as the warmth radiated down to their empty tummies.

Our family was one who also participated in these collections of the black & blue nuggets. We were more luckier then most kids in the neighborhood. We would get a hot meal plus the mug of hot chocolate with a marshmallow on top sprinkled with nutmeg & cinnamon.

If there's such a thing as soft luck then we shall zero in on the chicken's egg that come in all sizes & colors.

Like an egg, it can be Soft Boiled,
Poached, Hard Boiled, Pickled, Scrambled,
Fried & Dyed at Easter Time & also making
Egg & Olive Sandwiches, Egg Omelettes
& Deviled Eggs for a quick fix, etc., etc.

According to the egg theory we can make our luck become any way we want it to be, Hard or Soft.

If that egg sitting on the wall didn't fall then we wouldn't have to glue its pieces back together.

We could define Hard Luck as tough times when your really in need. Things do not go very well.

We could define Soft Luck as things given to you on a "Golden Platter." Everything you do seems to go well.

Guilty Or Not Guilty

There he stood with a guilty expression on his face. "What's your name?" asked the Judge. "Starving Andy" said the accused. The Judge asked him, "Well Starving Andy," "How do you plea of the charges that you stole the elderly lady's grocery bag in a store & ate half of what was in it in front of many, many witnesses?"

Then his expression changed for the worse and he replied, "Guilty your honor due to very, very personnel pain reasons."

His lawyer quickly intercepted & said, "We change that plea to not guilty your honor due to abnormal hunger pains." & we'll prove to the court that the evidence will bear the truth of the matter & furthermore the only evidence is that bag of half eaten fruit she's holding on her lap.

"Bring up your first witness" said the Judge. The lawyer replied, "I only have one witness your honor & that is the accused himself." "Very well, take the stand."

"Tell your story," said the judge.

"Well your honor, I followed the lady in the store to see what she was buying & low & behold she bought raisins, grapes, prunes, plums. That was the stuff I needed my doctor said to relieve my stomach problem."

Just then there was a loud roar, the elderly woman flew out of the courtroom, dropping the bag of fruit as she headed for the restrooms saying "Oh the hell with it, let him go, I can see now why he stole my bag of fruit."

"Case dismissed!" "Release the prisoner," said the Judge.

"Ahhh, I'm free again," said Starving Andy. He quickly picked up the bag of goodies & quickly consumed the rest of the fruit as he jet propelled himself out of the courtroom to a more comfy place.

Ancestors

I never knew what an Ancestor was. I thought it was somebody's sister.
Or was it the ancestor, the family's black sheep with an incurable blister.

Oh yes, every family had a skeleton in the closet who was the black sheep.
If you searched his or her history you would have to dwell ever so deep.

A photo of the Matriarch of the family with a stern steady glare.
She was majestic, with old fashioned clothes & with a bob of gray hair.

I never knew her, but her photograph left me with an emotional state.
I would look at her image, think of her, without love nor with hate.

She bore eight sons, two who died and six who I knew.
My father was one of them who raised me strong & true.

Eventually all the brothers passed away & we all said goodbye.
Knowing them was a pleasure in my lifetime I breathe with a sigh.

How far does one go back in time to search the family tree.
Names, places, dates & in cemeteries, the stones we see.

Reading their epitaphs, we will all learn about their life.
Those married with children, & husband & wife.

Hi Grandpa Joe, can you help me out? I'm doing the Family's history.
How come all the men have the same names in the church's ministry?

I said, "They are named after their families, Saints and each other.
Too numerous to mention, too difficult to research and don't even bother.

We did not choose them, they came before us.
So we must accept them without any fuss.

Ancestral sadness reaches our eyes as we learn more about our kin.
We dig up all kinds of stories & where they all have been.

What they have accomplished in their very short life span.
Makes us think & wonder about our life too, if we can.

The Heavy Cross

At first it was a device used by artisans
Constructing buildings by the town's partisans.

It was a useful idea in its times,
Its meaning was songful and with rhymes.

At first its purpose was good.
Its meaning of art was understood.

It stood upright with a transverse piece,
Then its useful meaning would come to cease.

Then came the cross,
Bearing no meaning, it was at a loss.

It would be used only for crucifixion
In times of ignorance, pain with much affliction.

In the ages of ignorance, sometimes turned upside down
Beggars & robbers were pinned, it made the populace frown.

People would see how this torture was used,
How their friends, families were being so abused.

It was made out of wood, heavy as can be
It was in the shape of a cross you see.

It was known as "The Heavy Cross"
And was only to carried by our "Heavenly Boss."

What kind of wood was it? I did not know at first.
Perhaps a tree of today, quenching its' thirst.

continues on next page...

The Heavy Cross

It did its sinful deed as everyone knows,
Hammered nails with striking blows.

The Cross from the Olive Tree
Was made from its wood for thee.

It was short in size, not very tall.
At eye level, Romans had lots of gall.

Fragments of wood on nails
Was proof for all that fails.

Using its oils for soothing taste,
Was the Crucification done in haste?

The heavy cross is remembered by all
For all our dastardly sins, He took the fall.

It was not the Cross of the crossed eyed bear
As if cursed by those who would dare.

How cross can the bear be when cornered by foes
From nagging forces hurled by painful blows.

But the man on the cross would forgive all.
Crucified on the heavy cross was so tall.

The "Rugged Cross", The Wooden Cross, The Iron Cross,
All over the world in the graveyards as they gather moss,

Reminding us how heavy the cross is that we all would bear
Giving us love by only one man who would dare to preach & share.

Amen

Best Things Are Free

Our very own life is free, a gift from God.
Whether your're a twin or one in a pod.
Free air that we breath & water that we drink
Goes through us in like a flash and a wink.
What we see, in our minds is to keep.
So beautiful the Earth, Sun & Moon, makes us weep.
Nature's beautiful wonderments are free to one & all.
Viewing the monuments makes us feel strong & tall.
Our children are the greatest gifts that's free.
Watching them grow to be we'll will wait & see.
Yes, the best things in life are free,
Just like nature's bird & the bee.

The following poem was inspired to me
by Hal Sachs

Gleaming Tree

It shines, it gleams
And dances like moonbeams.
Oh, how the tree does glow.

Changing hues as it turns,
Sprinkling colors as it yearns,
As if to say, "Please watch my show."

A gift of love cherished by all
Makes you heed its beckon call,
Of its perpetual spin ever so slow.

Its tiny lights scattered around tree,
Chasing colors for you and me.
Its meaning is magical and that we know.

Homeless

If your homeless, you will feel helpless.
If your homeless, you have no job.
If your homeless, you feel penniless.
If your homeless, you may have a box for a home.
If your homeless, you may feel worthless.
If your homeless, you have no place to go to.
If your homeless, you have no shoes under the bed.
If your homeless, you lose your self esteem.
If your homeless, you may become a beggar.
If your homeless, this story goes on & on & on.

The Homeless Bum

I have no job, I have no skills
My excuse is eating pills.
My brain is cooked.
And I've been hooked.
I get my traits from my drunken pappy.
And that's why I'm so darn happy.
He brought me up to steal & beg.
Stealing beer form the tap or a keg.
Yes, I have no skills
Yes, I have no bills.
In fact I have nothing to give.
Everything goes through me like a sieve.
This is the life I choose,
I never win, I just lose.
But still I'm a happy man.
Until the S--- / blankity blank hits the fan.
I do not compare my worldly woes.
To a successful person who knows,
I'm just a bum taking the daily tours.
I have the excuses, so what's yours?
So next time you see me on the street
Holding up my sign when we meet.
"I'm a just Bum" says on my sign
"A penny or two will do just fine."

Job...?

When you think of a Job, do you think of the "Book of Job" that in the Bible? Or are you thinking of a working job that you need money so badly to pay your bills?

One day I was walking home when a car stopped & friend of mine said, "Hey Joe, where you going?" I said, "Going home." He said, "Hop in, I'll give you a lift."

"Nice car, when did you get it?" " A couple of weeks ago." "Must have cost a lot, huh?" He said, "Well I got a job & I can pay for it, payments, you know, it'll take some time."

My friend Tom was well dressed & was happy. He always had nice things to say to you. He was a real gentleman.

"What do you owe your success to?" He immediately said,

"Hard work & sharing your wealth with the church, thanking the Lord for the things I have."

When I got home, I started to pray & pray. Telling the Lord I needed a job to get the things I wanted, a car, nice clothes, girls, happy times.I did this for several weeks and nothing.

I finally went to church and consulted a priest. I told him about my friend & what I was doing to fulfill my destiny.

He listened & said, "Things don't don't come free on a silver platter, you must work hard for the things you want."

You can pray all you want. He is listening but you have to help yourself to get the things you want. First you must serve him and the bounty will come you way.

Later, as time went by & with hard work, I too was able to raise a family in a new house. I guess you have to be humble and share you good fortune.

If you stand still & let life go by you will get nothing.

If you hang on to life & work hard work, You will succeed.

Be smart, save your money, hang on tight.
For you'll never know what's in sight.
Your job may last & maybe not,
That pile of dough is all you got.
If you make it your career your taking a chance.
If you lose it it may be your last dance.
Jobs come and go, now ain't that the truth.
Just like when you lose a tooth.

Countryside Fields

Driving through the countryside in Richfield Springs made me feel free just like animals that are there. The roving horses, rabbits, deer and flying birds give you sense of freedom.

The flowing fields in the winds made the hills come to life. The plush golden and purple carpets swaying with rhythmical gusts of wind has a tendency to hypnotize you.

Walking through the fields of corn, wheat, rye, clover and the natural instillment of nature's endowments made you feel rich with happiness and calming of one's mind. The natural vibrations of the movements, colors and its familiar smells that you grow up with.

As you walk you are overcome by a dreamy sensation of warmth and stillness. It is here you can relax in such a way that nature becomes your mentor.

Fields

Many Fields of Dreams come to mind,
And searching for them you may find.
Fields of Gold in the days of the 'Rush'
Kept secret by its owners claim with a hush.
If an Oil Field is what you want to make you rich,
Then you must drill a hole in that murky ditch.
If you strike the fields with a surging gush
Oil spouts up and its fountains rush.
Does baseball come to mind about the ball and the bat,
As you sit to enjoy with sun glasses and a hat.
The baseball field is a diamond shape
Ninety feet from home to first measured by a tape.
Bean fields, strawberry fields of all sorts
Food products imported from all foreign ports.
So when you see a field, think of what it can do.
Making you healthy, yielding its richness to you.

Names

Names, names,
Is it Jessie or James?
If you're an outlaw you play the game,
Robbing banks to gain your fame.

Names, names,
Is it Matilda for the dames?
Or the Shrew you must tame,
Or maybe its just a game.

Names, names,
Mine is Soldano,
Italian meaning, Soldier that tames,
Keeping order, is the soldier's aims.

Names, names,
Mine is Joseph & I'm no saint,
I'm on the street corner, looking at dames.
When the girls look at me, they all faint.

Naming a baby is easy to do.
You can call it Clem or Sue.
The list is endless, it has many a name.
Different names, but not two the same.

Nature's Little Sapling

Dear 'Little Sapling' embedded in the earth,
as your roots search for the liquid of life, quenching your
perpetual thirst.

Drink little one, "I Love You," drink to your heart's content
as the sun works its magic, turning your leaves into colorful
lush greenery.

The winds mingle among your branches, your leaves
shimmer under the sun.

Nature has her way of satisfying you pains of hunger.

The rings of age will be bestowed upon thee as you grow
older, taller and stronger.

Yes dear one, you will live to a ripe old age.
Your bark may wrinkle and peel without pain or rage,

You will have many friends to keep you company as your
seeds will be hurled far away by the friendly winds.

Landing where they may, it will be future homes to some.
But for others, little saplings will evolve into beautiful lush
forests giving homes to nature's wild life and yes, more little
saplings.

So when your're strolling in the countryside and see a
little sapling struggling for survival, bend down, look at it, it
will understand what you are imagining how it will look when
mother nature nurtures it into an earthly tall, spreading
beauty of a wooden majestic giant of an oak tree.

Ah yes, all plants sway with the rhythms of the winds and
the rains.

They do have feelings just like us and just think, in their
own way they make us also grow tall and strong.

Love is a true feeling of affection
    & compassion toward one another.
Over the years this feeling rears
    families into future generations.
Virility is in the Genes
    of the masculine beholder.
Everyone who possess love
    may celebrate it on Valentine's Day

Love spins the world around,
With human feelings but no sound.
Your hearts will know if your're in love.
And so does Cupid from way above.

He places an arrow in the bow,
And aims it right at her handsome beau.
The mark is true as it strikes home.
And she knows that he will no longer roam.

His eyes are just for her,
His love for her makes her purr.
They are caught in Cupid's web
Their Love will never ebb.

Love is happy & wonderful & not so tragic
To some, it's like living in a land of magic.
Love has many forms & comes in many ways,
Just like our Sun with its magical rays.

Judgement Day

Judgement day is offered to you by your family and peers.
Each day when you awake, you should have no fears.
You may judge others or they may judge you.
Your very existence, your life goes on what can you do.

You are one of twelve sitting on the jury,
The one being judged is fidgety with worry.
He sits in judgement, his case is heard,
Will he be imprisoned or fly like a bird?

Who is to judge you when you do right or wrong.
People are quick with an axe, it doesn't take long.
They'll chop you down for if they don't understand.
So we leave that up to the Judge with a gavel in hand.

You may stand in judgement in your everyday life.
If you're married & do wrong you must face your wife.
If you help people especially those who are in need,
You will be judged as a nice person who takes the lead.

When you die you'll be known as that good guy.
But you still must face your maker way up in the sky.
You will try to bust through that white pearly gate.
But first you must stand in Judgement with love nor hate.

If you're judged good on one hand and bad on the other.
Then you'll know that feathered Angel is not you brother.
You'll be so judged to go downstairs and ring that lowly bell,
To meet your true maker, who is the devil in hell.

Choices

Going through life, there will be many choices.
Your mind will be filled with many voices.
It's a push & pull game with decisions to make
If your choice is wrong, then your game will break.

If you had a choice would you choose a different kin?
Even if one of them was an embarrassing has-been.
What about siblings, what about mom & dad?
Now if your choice came true, wouldn't that be sad?

What choice do I have, If I'm just a fool?
I'm that screw-up who quit school.
My choices are far in between the cracks of success
No matter what, I must take any job no less.

How many times have bought your friends a gift?
And you just couldn't make up your mind, get the drift?
So many choices to choose from, what am I to buy?
It's your choice, make up your mind, a shirt or a tie?

Some choices are good and some are bad.
It's like taking a chance, if you win you're glad.
So when you say to others, "Do I have a choice?"
Just listen to your conscious with that inner voice.

Free Style

Ah, To be Free!
At the tender age of three.
Then you grew up in 'Golden Style,'
As the Pharaoh, you cruised the Nile.

Just how free is your style?
Are rules changed with a turn of the dial?
Or are you cramped with burdened rules,
With all those necessary tools?

True art style has rigid forms,
But are broken in College Dorms.
A student writes best when thinking free.
He has his own style, original as can be.

No matter what in life all that we do,
Dancing, singing, its Art comes to you.
Whether its true to form or free as the wind.
Your Free Style will hail again & again.

The breast stroke is a heavy pace.
It will always be kept in place.
Free Style swimming is your race,
If you don't win, you will lose face.

So, if Free Style is your cup of tea,
Try to win & be the best you see,
Then you can walk in style with head up high.
Gaining self esteem as you breath with a sigh.

House Keeper

You have a house & you're its keeper.
Sometimes the chores get deeper & deeper.
As a house keeper you do all the cooking.
You may burn the toast when no one's looking.

Married or not you should keep house.
And setting a trap to catch the mouse.
Having a pest free place to live in.
If you bathe everyday that's no sin.

You may be a butler or you may be a maid.
You mop the floors until they fade.
You keep the house at its very best.
After all it is your little love nest.

Things will get better.
Do things by the letter.
Have fun with the new born pup,
And fry your eggs sunny-side up.

Your the boss, your the house keeper
Halloween is coming, Jeepers-Creepers
So be nice to the Kids, give them candy
Your house wont be tricked and that's dandy.

So keep your house nice and clean
Polish your wares until they gleam.
Rake the leaves, mow the lawn.
You may have to work until early dawn.

A Christmas Dream

A Christmas Dream is what we wish.
The tree is trimmed with heavenly bliss.
Children asleep within their dreams,
Dancing on silver moonbeams.

Velvet red & snowy white
Venturing into the magical night.
Snowy white & velvet red
He's plump & round & well fed.

Sparkling stars light his way
Into the night a speeding sleigh.
All the toys now under the tree,
One for you & one for me.

Fluffy white & crimson red,
A tassel cap on his head.
Quiet as a mouse & swift as a deer,
Jolly old Nick is finally here.

His bulging bag is full of wishes
For mom it may be a set of dishes,
For dad it may be a shirt or tie,
Children were so happy, they could cry.

Little children looking up high.
At the silver streak in the sky
Waving to Santa & saying goodbye.
"Next year we'll see you" they said with a sigh.

The Witch Is Brewing

The witch is brewing a magic spell,
It's Halloween night & monsters dwell.
Cursing people with the wave of her hand.
As she rides her broomstick over the land.

Her black cat is hissing, owls are hooting.
Ghouls awake, their children are looting
Dancing witches their bats are flying.
Spirits & Vampires awaken after dying.

A favorite costume is a child's delight,
It may be pretty or ugly, but oh what a sight
A knock on the door, "Trick or Treat."
The door opens, lots of candy ever so sweet.

As the night passes, the children go home.
But Ghosts & Goblins & Spirits still roam.
The sun is rising & they too go to sleep.
To their earthly beds that were dug ever so deep.

But the Witch is still cursing, "I'll see you next year!"
To all my little pretties, "I'll scare you, never fear."
Her pot still boils & many Spells she will weave
To cast them on all the children on Halloween Eve.

Halloween

To all of you, I'm saying Booooo!
To all you Poets, you know Whooooo
I'm writing this poem just for Yooooooou!
Let's go Trick or Treating at the Zooooooo!

We're sitting & its not a round table
Let me tell you about a Halloween Fable.
I'm going to scare you out of your wits.
I'm going to cut you up into little bits.

Yes, I'm dressed up as the Chain-Sawman
And my trusty Chainsaw hums like a fan.
As I cut up tomb stones it creates a spark.
It lights up the night, it's no longer dark.

Halloween always gets the best of me,
I'm part of a weird-crazy-weirdo-scary clan you see.
If I cut off part of your body you wont care.
I'm only trying to give you a tiny little scare.

So when you go home to your mommy dear
And she sees you with no arms, never fear.
I broke my chainsaw and broke its gear.
If you think that's something just wait till next year.

Famous Day
— Yet Tragic —
Can You Remember
What Were You Doing?
"Well I do...by Joe Soldano"

The Assassination of John F. Kennedy
35th President of the United States

On a bright sunny day I was painting the living room.
Little did I know It was going to be "The Day Of Doom".
Up from the cellar came the telephone guy.
Shouting President Kennedy was shot & may die.

A bullet with blood on it found its mark
Finding its victim like a blood thirsty shark.
Yes the telephone guy was right John did die.
And America started grieving with tears in their eye.

Friday, Nov. 22, 1963, in Dallas, Texas, the Lone Star State,
Struck squarely in the head, no bulletproof dome, it was too late.
The second bullet struck Govenenor Connaly sitting by his side.
Just like the President who struck, there was no place to hide.

"The Day Of Doom", if you can remember
It took place in the month of November.
On television sets the grisly scene was shown all day,
For we lost our President, who's going to pay?

Nice Teachers
and
Bad Teachers

There's always the Good and there is always the Bad,
Now take some teachers, some were the best I've ever had.
We'll start with the bad ones who left scars in my brain.
They scolded & tormented & left me with much pain.

Now let's take the good ones who I shall always remember.
Even in winter, summer and even the month of December.
Mr. Bughental was my art teacher he taught me well.
He put Ideas in my mind that ring my bell.

My music teachers were always pleasant and nice
Not like some teachers who were cold like ice.
Some were very old, senile and naturally mean
Maybe they couldn't help themselves it would seam.

If a teacher was nice you would always learn.
If a teacher was mean, you felt a slow burn.
My Music Professor, "Mike" was a great guy
He always feeds me Wine, Cheese & Tomato Pie.
(or Pizza)

My Body Parts

Did you ever think that the organs in your body have value?... If they are healthy and in good condition, then you can reap the crops. I mean money wise.

There is a long waiting list for livers, kidneys etc.

So next time you go to the meat market to buy your groceries and see these items in meat cases, just think what a waste it is to eat them.

An Ode To My Body Parts

My brain is incased within my head.
It needs plenty of rest when I go to bed.
My bones keep my body straight and tall.
But they will break if I have a bad fall.

My trusty fingers are a joy to me,
They are connected to my hands you see.
Their movements make for dancing fingers.
On wedding days they become finger ringers.

My arms need plenty of elbow room.
When I sweep the floor with a broom.
My legs are good for running and walking
They do their chores without even squawking.

All my body parts, I need them so.
Going through life I surely know.
I think I'm put together fairly well.
And with that said I feel swell.

Without my heart my days will be over.
My daily tours, I can no longer rover,
And not to mention my private parts
Like Banana Splits & Strawberry tarts.

Thanksgiving

Let's give thanks to the Pilgrims on this day.
They were the one who forged the way.
They made it so to say the least.
So we could sit & enjoy the feast.

Let's give thanks for the living.
Let's give thanks for the giving.
The table is set with turkey & dressing.
So eat your food with God's Blessing.

Indian "Squanto" taught Pilgrims to plant seeds
And taught the children to make beads.
He was a friendly Indian & taught his ways
And made it easier for the coming days.

The Corn was new, popcorn looked liked snow
Warm to the touch, eaten the children would grow.
The Indians brought them Turkeys & good will,
It was free to the Pilgrims & there was no bill.

There was turkey, chestnuts, yams & popcorn,
Everyone came to the table with the sound of a horn.
The feast is on, lots of food & the horn of plenty.
Indians stood guard like a protective sentry.

The tablecloth is adorned with lace.
The dishes are prepared with loving care
And Turkey's on the table for all to share.
Thanksgiving is the day to say Grace.

Into The Future

Riding the winds on beams light
As I journey into the future holding tight
Gasping & holding with all my might
Am I to experience a wondrous sight?
Looking at my future in a crystal ball.
What's in store for me, can I have it all?
Will I ride high or have a fall?
Will my journey stop & stall?

If I crack the glass, will my future hold?
Probably not, for it is told, I broke the mold.
So I built a time machine just to see
If I could venture into that celestial sea.
I Plugged it in & turned it on & set the controls to a future date
When I arrived, nothing there, the land was bare, was I too late?
I made a U turn & headed back, my time machine is working great.
Got back home, made a few calculations, off again to check my fate.

I flew into the future to see what's really in store for me.
When I got there I was so successful that I was happy as an be.
All my great-grand-kids have kids of their own.
They are all grown up & have their own cell phone.
Just like kids today, they like to gab away
Anyway we'll check on them another day.
I'm still flying into the future, how far can I go?
All my family is fading away, where are they? I don't know.

But the phone bill is getting larger, & there's no one to pay.
The bill is now shredded & scattered like hay.
My future has no future, it has faded away,
I went to far, can't get back to my original day.
My success is gone there is nothing there,
My future has passed, why did I dare?
I took this trip, it just had to done.
But really it wasn't much fun.

Infinity has played its part on this hideous ride.
There is no end to my future, no place to hide.
But wait, there is some light, I'll ride its beam.
I made it back, guess what? It was only a dream.

Changing Times

No matter what time it is when you look a a clock.
The hands revolve around its block.
The block meaning a dial for its face
Always smiling at you with its steady pace.

Never stopping, just ticking away,
Changing seconds, minutes & hours into a day.
It could be electric or a self-wind,
And It only has one thing in mind.

When I think of changing times.
I think of poetry that always rhymes.
I don't think of the world's political reasons,
I only think of the 4 changing seasons.

With a tick of the clock, time advances ahead.
The past has gone, & it is now instead.
Times change for the worse or for the better,
And we all make due of it right to the letter.

There's the past, there's the now & what's to come?
It sounds like a Christmas story for some.
Old fashioned ways are of the past,
Inventors knew they would not last.

Modern times are here to stay
But the past did have its way,
The memories of it still linger on
Remember the clothes we used to don?

History repeats itself & keeping that in mind.
We dig for riches & the treasures that we may find.
Yes times are changing & probably for the best,
For the believers, the nonbelievers & all the rest.

Winter

Beautiful crystals falling as snow.
Reflecting light from towns below.

Different snowflakes spun by Jack Frost
They scatter around & even get lost.

Later they gleam under the moonlight,
And Jack admires the beautiful sight.

The first snow fall reminds of the Season's Winter,
But do not slip & fall or you'll wear a splinter.

Let's do some ice skating but please do not fall.
Riding toboggans, sleigh rides & skiing for all

But Winter gets cold with its shivering blast
You wear heavy clothes hoping it won't last.

Hurling snowballs is the game to play.
Making snowmen makes one happy & gay.

Frost bitten toes & frost bitten faces,
They don't care, ther're off to the races.

The winner gets a trophy for being first.
Then tips his head to quench his thirst.

It reminds us of the Holiday that is yet to come.
We will all have a cheer drinking buttered rum.

Rumors

Its a funny thing about rumors
No we're not talking about folks with tumors.
That starts out small & grows up big.
Maybe to the size of an 18 wheel rig.

The truth could end up growing into being lies.
Lies could end up in a divorce couple who had ties.
Sometimes the subject could be way off course.
That is not relying on its original truthful source.

A rumor can be twisted or untwisted just a tad,
And believe me that could be really bad.
Want to make up a rumor, try this for size.
If that guy started drinking it would be his demise.

He's a good guy, I've never seen take a drink in his life.
How do you know maybe he really does drink.
Yeah maybe that's why he has a certain stink.
Could be, could be, he may be on the edge of a brink.

I did see him at a bar once,
Probably drunker than a dunce.
I think he steals too to say the least.
And just think he wanted to be a priest.

To bend the truth like some people do
Makes the rumor stick like glue.
First impressions always stick with us.
But we like to twist that too & make a fuss.

So next time you hear rumor, listen with your ears
It could be about you or your friendly peers.
We all like to gossip & the truth may unfold.
Into a rumor that was so wickedly told.

Best Christmas Gift

I must have been 5 or 6 years old at the time.
My family didn't have much, not even a dime.
We were on Welfare like a lot of people in our town.
No work, nothing to do, just knocking around.

But it was the holiday season & Christmas was here,
Will Santa visit our house with his reindeer?
My Aunt had a Christmas Tree, so green & tall.
And its beauty was to be shared by all.

I ran downstairs to see the Christmas Tree.
All the presents underneath were free.
One for you & a surprise for me.
It came in a box, heavy as can be.

I read the card, it said for Junior, initialed JR
I was beaming just like a movie star.
I ripped open the package as fast as I could.
What could be in it, chunks of coal or chunks of wood?

To my surprise it wa a wind-up Choo-Choo Train.
Oh what a joy, glad it wasn't a new puppy to train.
It was a gift from my lovable Grandma,
And also marked on it was from Grandpa.

The train was the only toy I got.
But I did get a shirt & a tie to knot.
The train went around & around
On an oval track making a whirling sound.

I had the happiest Christmas that year,
Remembering the train from Grandma dear.
I'll never forget, it was the best gift I ever got
And that's the truth, I'll kid you not.

                                                JR

Curiosity

You all heard the phrase,
"Curiosity killed the cat."
"But satisfaction brought it back."
Now just exactly what does that mean?

Does Curiosity really kill?
No, their just nosy & they want their fill.
What are they talking bout? Are they talking about me?
Their blasted Gossiping is really killing me you see."

If curiosity killed me, can I ever really come back?
Were they satisfied, can I unzipped the body sack?
We're all creatures of curiosity, we can't help it.
Because noses are in front of our head we sniff a bit.

A little sniff here, a little sniff there.
Its none of our business, do we really care?
Are we really satisfied of what we hear?
Remember our curiosity is still sniffing, never fear.

Insanity or Sanity

Are you insane if you lose your mind?
All your leanings you will never find.
You are now alone, you are left behind.
Your gray matter is twisted & in a bind.

Your ego has left & so has your vainity.
As it enters the threshold of insanity.
It is the dark side for one to bear
As you hide alone in your darkened lair.

On the other hand, are you sane & comprehend,
From all your school classes you did attend.
You live a normal life but still you wonder.
That someday your mind may falter & blunder.

Your sainity is yours alone to keep & treasure.
To live each day with happiness & all its pleasure.
Your mind is unlocked with its learning gift.
Be thankful your mind is stable & will never drift.

After Christmas Sales

Why do stores always have Christmas Sales?
Why do we run to the stores wagging our tails?
It's because there's always sales after Christmas day.
And we're were trained by department stores to be that way.
It is because the stores have us just where they want us.
We bang in doors, stampede like crazy making lots of fuss.
Prices should be reduced throughout the year.
Then we would buy goods without fuss & fear.
That will never happen my friends because of the dollar
They don't care what you buy even if you scream & holler.
So after Christmas Day there will always be sales.
Company policy rules, sell the stock, that's what prevails

New Years Eve

New Year wishes to you who are gathered around this table.
We listened to all of you Poets whether they be fact or fable.
Let the New Year bring your ideas to us & we will see,
If your prose or poetry is written about you or me.
We used to toast the New Year in.
We don't do that anymore, what a sin.
We used to go night clubbing, when Joe played Gigs.
We used to dance to fox trots, waltzes, tangos & Jigs.
Dolores is sound asleep, I'll sit up & watch TV
To bring in the New Year with just myself & me.
We're older, tired & wiser now we lost that zip.
But we'll celebrate the New Year with a little nip.
So upon closing my friends, get ready for our next meetings,
Happy New Year to you with wonderful season's greetings.

Things We Used To Do,
That We Don't Do Now

Money, money changed our views.
Bad economy is in the news.
Things we used to do that we don't do now,
Because of that Almighty buck, how low must we bow.

When we dined out it was expensive meals.
Now its beans, popcorn & meals on wheels.
Age is part of our life style now.
But we still drink milk from Elsie the cow.

We used to smoke many, many years past.
We stopped and were glad it didn't last.
Drinking & gambling was part of my vice.
Resolutions change with the roll of the dice.

No more gambling, no more drinking,
What in the world was I thinking.
I used to go out with the boys & have lots of fun.
Now I'm a house husband, keeping me on the run.

What Important Things In 2009?

In 2,009 my blood was checked for corpuscles of red.
I had too much iron & my heart skipped a beat, I wasn't dead.
Doc told me I was anemic, now what's my fate?
I worried so much, I lost lots of weight.

You got too much iron in your blood,
No red wine for you or it may turn into mud.
Don't worry he said, as long as you're well fed.
Eat all kinds of food, for your corpuscles of red.

Then in the same year of 2,000 & nine
My doctor said, "Do this procedure & you'll be fine."
It took me several to make up my mind.
I was afraid of what they would find.

After six weeks the day finally came.
At the hospital, they called out my name.
They told me what to expect, they put me to sleep.
I was a good patient, I made no sound, not even a peep.

The doctor checked me out, found nothing, I was OK.
He said, "the procedure was good for 10 years to the day.
I'll be 91 then, maybe in good health, but will I be free?
No, I guess I'll have to look forward to my next colonoscopy.

Lost Poem

They say to write it down so you you won't forget.
That's just what I did, bit by bit.

But the poem I wrote upon the page,
Many years later faded with age.

I tried to read it but could not,
What its topic was, I forgot.

Was it a master piece, I've written down,
Trying to remember makes me frown.

I searched & searched my mind to find,
My poem is gone it has left my mind.

Maybe someday it may come back to me.
I'm still searching, where can it be?

Write It Down So You Won't Forget It

I forgot to write down the idea I thought about today,
So I think I'll try to remember it tomorrow,
What was it about, can't remember, what can I say.
If I remember it, there won't be so much sorrow

Write it down so you won't forget, that's a great rule.
And if you forget it, who's fault is it?
Don't be stubborn just like a donkey or a mule
Who likes to neigh, jump & have a fit.

Your prose & poetry may be great in your mind,
But if its not in black & write who can read it & say.
If written down, it will be listed for people to find.
Then they'll read it, recite it in their own way.

So next time your get an Idea that you think is great,
Grab a pad & pencil & just write it down
It may be night time & may be getting late.
But at least it'll be there & then you won't frown.

Spooks

The night comes with all its presence
and stirring of the flukes,
The 31st of October is here
and gives way to the howling Spooks.
Or it may any day
to pick on people just to spook,
We'll get them so nervous,
they'll bend over sick and puke.
The ghosts of war with its flying spooks
We'll not forget the war of the atomic nukes
An Asian city wiped out with a mighty blast
Now lives with a horrifying past.
The Poltergeist is a nagging creation
of the devil full of sins
Living in the bowels of the earth
in blackened coal bins
Sending the ghost that manifests itself
by noises that ring in your ear.
His creation of disorder,
rapping on doors to cause you fear.

Dreams

Some times I'm lost in a dream.
There's no light, no life, what does it mean.
The stillness and emptiness makes me wonder,
There's no weather here, no sound of thunder.

No glimmer of moonbeams, no sun showers.
No trees, no grass, no brooks, no flowers.
No stars that twinkle, no sparkles that gleam.
Am I trapped here forever, what does it mean.

No wind on my face, I don't feel a thing.
No music here, cannot even sing.
I can not hear my voice, I can not talk,
I can not see a path on which to walk.

If I don't wake up, what does this mean.
I cannot cry, should I redeem.
All my sins of the past,
Or must I stay here, steady and fast.

Am I to stay forever in this blackened hell,
I can not scream or even yell.
But wait, something is going on in my ear,
There is a clamor of sound, I can hear.

continues on next page...

Dreams

I was scared with the worst of fears.
But the morning sounds delighted my ears
I felt I was bound by a strangling rope,
I struggled to move. Is there still hope?

So I slapped my face as hard as I could,
My body and mind understood.
I quickly arose from out of my bed,
Was it the closest to being dead.

My dreams are getting better,
So I'll write them down in this letter,
I'm still trying to get it all together,
With sweet smells
from flowers and heather.

My dreams are now full of spice,
With colorful skies and fields of rice.
People will marry as church bells ring
Happiness is here, now I can sing.

Favorite Place

My favorite place does not exist.
I try to think of it, I can not resist.

Is it tucked away, way back in my mind.
Trying to retrieve it, I can not find.

Is it a figment of my imagination?
Or is it just a conglomeration?

Is it a place in another land.
Or embedded in shores of sand.

Could it be "Shangrala"
or
"UTOPIA" thats talked about.
To get there we must take an imaginary route.

After finding it, will it please me?
This could in fact be my favorite you see.

I've often thought of a favorite place.
To get away from this boisterous race.

If I was a pilot it could be the sky,
Flying like an Eagle way up high.

continues on next page...

Favorite Place

If I was a fish, it would be the ocean.
What an idea, what a notion.

I'd swim about to see all my friends,
And peering at me through their lens.

So my favorite place is anyplace I want it to be.
Maybe its a golf course with the ball on a tee.

Maybe to play the piano in Carnegie Hall.
Boy, if that was the case I'd have a ball.

Well enough of favorite places,
I'm off to the races.

I'm off to the downs,
someplace out of town.

If I ever find that favorite place,
I'm sure to make it my home base.

So I think my home is my favorite spot
All decorated with frilly lace and polka dot.

Valentines Day Is For My Wife Dolores

On Valentine's Day
it is very easy for me to write down this poem.
My wife and I got married on this day
when Cupid's arrow was driven home.
Dolores & I picked this day 'cause
Valentine's Day is so easy to remember.
It falls upon February 14th, not the month of
November or the month of September.

The first year it was 1 heart
and now the total is 58 hearts.
It took Cupid a total of 58 years
throwing his traditional loving darts.
The red heart is the symbol
that is adorned on most Valentine Cards.
As they are protected by
St. Valentine's Angelic Heavenly Guards.

Roses are red, violets are blue, I give my love to you.
Many sayings are written on this day from you know who.
Love, love, love that is what Valentines Day means.
Taking your girl or beau to the downtown's many scenes.

A bouquet of red or pink roses
will make her happy as can be.
Or maybe a tie & a kiss
will make him lovable because of thee.

continues on next page...

Valentines Day Is For My Wife Dolores

Its one of the busiest flower days
that all florists will surely know.
And every year the
"Lovable Red Rose" will grow and grow.

The symbolic heart is the core of a male's life.
Its inner meaning is destined to take himself a wife.
The heart's color of red is symbolic of the blood within,
And that is where Valentines Day will always begin.

Color White is a symbol of purity as it should be.
The bridal gown of white satin with a veil to hide and see.
All the spectators will witness to this holy marriage,
As happy days will be in store for the babe in a carriage.

The female's heart is ready to serve & always will.
Its steady flow of life is meaningful but very still.
Yet on the other hand its fruits of life will always bear kin,
As our Children share love with happiness again and again.

So Happy Valentines Day to all of you who share this day
With candy hearts, flowers & pretty writings on cards that say.
"This box of delights will light up your eyes
as you feast on these treats
Given to you on Valentines Day
from my heart with rhythmical beats.

Dreams of Nightmares

Why is it that we can't remember that pleasant dream
we had last night that was filled with cake & ice cream,
happy times, bright ideas that comes to ones' mind.
When we awake we let them go & they remain behind.

But yet we can remember that scary nightmare dream
that was filled with terror that made you scream.
You know the ones that make you pull hairs out of your head
and in the morning you're so happy to get out of bed.

The old wise tales tell us a nightmare
may have an evil meaning
so true that we might carry it through life
and that is very demeaning.
If we dream of the dead, someone may die,
and some would believe that is a bold face lie.

It all depends who writes the book
is it true or false we'll take a look.
Some times it is opposite of what we dream,
get the drift you know what I mean.

Psychiatrists tell us our dreams are
our experiences from day to day.

How can that be if one dreams of
his or her demise what can one say.

So it must have been some else
who has died in your place with disguise.

When you awake you will be happy
of that nightmare you so despise.

Writing a Morning Poem

I got up this morning to write this poem,
To read for the Poets Society away from home.
Thinking about the things I did.
Last week that blew my lid.
Medical procedures for my wife.
Grocery shopping what a life.
Not to mention copying movies to disc.
The warning signs may put you at risk.
Its quite a world we live in with new electronic things.
People walking around as their earplugs sing.
So, I'll make this short, I'll read it you.
Don't you think what I wrote is true.

My Favorite Stars

It's hard to pick out a 'Favorite Star'
Because their distant is so very far.
Just like the bright north star,
That twinkles in the sky black as tar.
Many stars are in the Milky Way.
And please listen to what they say.
"To pick a movie star, female or male,
They are all great and all prevail."
A star is picked for the movie role,
And the Statue will be their goal.
Like all the stars in the Milky Way,
We may become a star some day.
We can only hope if this comes true.
So we can shine in the sky so blue.
Our favorite star is our very own sun.
So lets go to the movies and have fun.

Some of My Daily Routines

Upon getting up in the morning
After all that nightly snoring,
I hope today is not so boring.

Sprinkling water on my face
It's coolness will start my daily pace
Giving thanks with a morning grace.

I toast some bread & scramble eggs
Giving strength to my wobbling legs.
After when we are fed.
I wash the dishes & make the bed.

At the computer, I read my E-mail
I get lots of letters without fail.
At the piano I will play a song,
You may listen or sing-a-long.

Dashing to the grocers for something to eat
Walking the isles keeps me on my feet.
Buying items I wisely choose,
Just wholesome food & please, no booze.

In the evening we'll watch the Telly
Having Hors d' Oeuvres to fill the belly.
We'll catch the late news, then off to bed,
Remembering to set the clock 1 hour ahead.

Old Time Printing

As a printer, you had to know, What? Where? & When?
It was the 1st rule you would learned how to begin

You pull out letters out of a case & made a sign by hand,
After printing it, it will be distributed throughout the land.

We'll set our headline in bold face gothic 24 lines high,
Because it will be easy reading for the naked eye.

An inch would contain 6 picas or a total of 72 points.
Sometimes setting type was hard on the finger joints.

Our trusted tool was our pica stick.
We could set type quick, lickety split.

Pieces of type were hand picked from a California Job Case,
After setting up the form, it would be locked in an iron chase.

Then it would be placed on a printing press to print our signs.
That we laboriously hand picked, setting up lines after lines.

The old printing job shop was busy in those days.
It was noisy & printing got done without delays.

Cooling was done by huge electrical fans on hot summer days
You could call It was a sweat shop, heated by the sun rays.

At days end our hands were blackened with printers ink
And we would scrub them in a dirty old galvanized sink.

With black under the finger nails from that smelly printer's ink
And the odors in the shop on hot days would make you think.

That was old time printing that you very seldom see today.
Only to be seen in restored showcased versions on display.

Mysteries, Faces and Noises

When I think of Mysteries, Faces & Noises, Movies
come to mind very readily. Sound effects is one of the most
important aspects of movie watching.
　　Without it there would be no heart thumping surprises.
　　Close ups of mysterious people, with clamoring sounds
of musical noises is left up to your imagination of what is
about to happen..
　　Huge giant close-ups of the actors on the screen
together with shrilling music, cymbals crashing and the
noise from the roaring crowd makes your ticket worth
while. The mysterious plots of some stories makes you
gasp at times as you run to the rest room to hide.

Oh, the mysteries of a noisy scary face,
Hiding in some unknown mysterious place.
Scarring the living wits & daylight out of you
That's what the plot of a mystery can do.

Millions & millions of wrenching faces
Are screaming in mysterious places.
Their stories unfold as you read their books,
Noises & faces will sink in their hooks.

Taking hold of your mind deep within,
Who knows where their stories begin.
The ringing of sound grows stronger
In my brain, can't stand it no longer.

The mystery within is a living graveyard
The memories of thinking is very hard.
Of familiar noises & faces I once knew,
They are gone now except, but for a few.

Once Upon A Time

(Written at the spur of the moment at the Poet's meeting)

Once upon a time when I didn't have dime,
I think of peace and of the sublime.

I think of happy and sad times of my past,
That was ever so swift and did not last.

All my family helped me on my way,
Their advice I remember to this day.

I grew up so fast, as I gave it a whirl,
Did I ever have a chance in this twirling world?

Then Puppy love would entered my picture,
And soon to become a permanent fixture.

As I grew up and went on a date.
Mom always said don't come home too late.

Went to lots of picture shows and had lots of fun,
Ate lots of pizzas and lots of hot dog in a bun.

My piano lessons made me grow up so fine,
And later in high school it made me shine.

As I remember all the things I did
And all the troubles I would soon rid.

I am so glad that I'm able to recall my past
Of my memories that went by so very fast.

I'm happier now and that's a good sign,
That I'm able to find peace of mind.

I Am The World's Greatest Liar

I honestly & truly believe I am the worlds's greatest liar.
How's that you mean?

Well, I can make up stories that sound so true & mixed up,
that the listener or reader will believe every word of it.

I can take any subject & lie about it.
After all the're only words twisted just a trifle.

Now, take that salt shaker on the kitchen table,
empty it out on the surface.
Now look at it. It is now a pile of sugar.
I said its a pile of sugar, believe me, its a pile of sugar.
But don't taste it.

But if you do, it will taste as sweet as my lie.
It's like twisting the subject just a tad.

You still don't believe me. Mix it up with sugar & taste it.
Don't we cook & bake combining salt and sugar?
Just think of how many times you have mistaken salt for sugar.

Now take that little white lie
that passes up by.
It's not white at all, It's black.
It's painted all over your back.
We think of black that's blue
Believe me now that white lie is now true.

Could it be that I'm such a great liar, that whoever reads
my stories & believes in them are just gullible as I am.

Maybe its because people don't want to hear the truth.

So what do I do? . . . . *I LIE !* . . . .

My Favorite Summer

The day I would become a member of the Boys Club in Utica, N.Y. I remember one summer when the nights were hot and there no wind. We just moved into our new apartment.

I was a new kid on the block. I had no friends at this new location. Our apartment was a above a restaurant. It was a hangout for cigar smoking, guzzling beer and clam eaters.

Yes it smelled like cigars, beer and clams. Oh yes there were cockroaches too.

There was an old green, red & white parrot who lived in our the building. Sometimes the owner would put it out on the front porch and I would go to the cage and talk to the parrot. "Poly wants a cracker?" That was the way of communicating with the parrot. He had a small but clear vocabulary. I had lots of fun with it. He knew some naughty words too, I often wondered who thought him that.

I remember lots of kids were jumping over the fence next to the building to get to the Boys Club that was on the other side of the block. It was a shot cut. But I had access to the Boys Club in the back of the building that more or less was a private easement to the Club. The kids thought I was lucky. I quickly became friends with them. I felt much better.

Membership was free, but we had to pay a quarter for the thick plastic, maroon color card, that was lacquered to protect the printing and my name on it.

Being a member now I qualified for the summer camp in the Adirondack Mountains at Raquette Lake. It was near Mt. Macintire. I can't remember the name of the camp, but we'll call it Camp Macintire.

It was the first time I was away from my family all by by myself. I did get homesick but that soon passed. All the activities made me forget and I had lots of fun.

That night we all sat around the campfire roasting marshmallows and hot dogs & just having fun.

continues on next page...

My Favorite Summer

Then the camp leader would tell us stories about the forests and especially about the headless Indian that roamed the forest with no soul that rose up every night looking for his lost head. He would naturally scare anyone out of their wits who crossed his path.

Just then bushes and leaves would start to make cracking outlandish sounds as if they were screaming and everyone got scared. A giant headless Indian came running into the camp site and the fires lit him up like a phantom of the night. There were noisy Indians chasing him all over the place. All the kids were screaming and panic set in. Just then we were told to stop the whining. It was only a scene that was played out many times before. There was no Indian only a disguised leader and helpers having fun on our expense. Then we all laughed it off. The camp leader afterwards told us not to tell the new campers when they arrived because it would spoil it for everyone, so we kept it a secret.

The next morning we had breakfast and packed our gear. We were to mountain climbing. When we got to the top of the mountain I thought I would pluck a piece cloud out of the sky. The clouds were like thick fog just floating by. I was disappointed that I couldn't bring my Mom a piece of cloud.

The morning were chilly and the butter on the tables were hard. Couldn't spread in on a slice of bread. Then I thought maybe the ends of the loaves would be able to handle the spreading of the butter. It was there I got my Junior life saving patch. I had to swim an 1/8th of mile to one point to another in the lake. Had to tip over a canoe and get back in and bail out the water. I had to dive down 7 feet of water and retrieve weights that were about 5 feet apart.

We were taught how to save a drowning person who was panicking in the water. Never to face him head on. We would dive down in the water, grab his legs, turn him around and put him in an arm lock and swim him back to shore.

Thanks to the Boys Club of America, I grew up to be a responsible young fellow.

Birthday Parties, Balloons and Presents

Driving around the area I would see different colored balloons pinned to trees, doorways, front yards, campsites and other pin-able places.

Bright colored balloons for Happy Occasions, Graduations and Black & Purple for Sad Occasions.

Just recently on the corner of University & Park Blvd. there was a sad event. There were flowers and balloons, reminding us of a tragedy that took place there recently.

A boy on a bicycle was taken from from us due to a tragic accident. Speeding was the cause.

But on the other hand there are more happy events taking place every day around town reminding us of happy times and happy memories.

It's your birthday and you have present to unwrap.

Oh how joyful it can be to tear the wrappings and string to get at that wanting treasure.

Sometimes its your wish come true and sometimes its not. You make the best of it.

But all in all you did have a Happy Birthday and you got lots of presents with all the floating balloons in the air.

I remember once, on the day of my Birthday, I went next door to visit my Aunt Rose. There were balloons and presents piled high. A large fancy birthday cake was the centerpiece. Oh, how happy I was to be reminded that it was my birthday.

But sadly to say when my eyes saw a little girl all dressed in colored silk and lace, with curly hair and all. It was her birthday to be honored instead.

I just had a couple of birthday parties celebrated in my honor so I very quickly swallowed my pride and ate some of her birthday cake & watched her tear open here presents with vigor.

So, I say the moral of this story is, "How much birthday cake can you really eat?"

I'm Always Thinking of
Something To Write....!

I'm always thinking of something to write,
My ideas comes best when I work at night.
Can not work in the dark, I must have light.
Otherwise I may lose my sight.

What shall I write about with pen in hand,
Should it be about mountains that rule our land,
Or at the beach as children play in the sand
Or just about life that is ever so grand.

All my poems are created for you to read,
In a comfortable chair thats all you'll need,
With a drink in one hand while smoking a weed
And take your time at your own leisurely speed.

I always rhyme words with vigor and zest.
Words from my brain thats where they nest.
My poems could be the very best
If they stand out above all the rest.

continues on next page...

I'm Always Thinking of
Something To Write....!

I carry a pencil, pen and a pad,
That's all I need and that makes me glad.
I'll write about something happy or bad.
About a gal who was jilted now so sad.

He was her beau, a handsome lad
Had all the trade marks of his dad.
He was conceited just a tad,
Now he pines for the gal he had.

I search and search until I find,
What ever ideas come in my mind,
What is the topic to be that's behind,
That sometimes puts me in a bind.

The end of this poem is coming near,
And I'll write it down without any fear.
So read this poem for all to hear.
As you smoke that weed and have a beer.

Dolores, my wife, is the author of the next 2 lines,
And this is what she writes as she pines.
"Think about a movie star's face,
This poem is not finished, so watch this space.

Then and Now
"This poem is a little on the humor side"

How do I begin this story, 'That was then'
I got away with everything way back when.
My story has changed and that is now
So please excuse if I take a bow.
I used to fit in a baby seat
Then I had such little feet.
Now that seat does not fit my belly
And my feet are huge and smelly.

I was a little handsome Brute.
I was so cuddly and cute.
I'm not cuddly and cute any more,
So when I sleep, boy do I snore.
It used to cost a dime to see a movie.
And I thought that was kind of groovy.
Now the ticket I buy is for an adult
And I have to take it below the belt.

A dime would buy a double-dip ice cream cone,
At the butchers' you could get Fido a free bone.
Now milk has gone up, hey gimme a break,
No more free bones, not even a steak.
We used to eat good, everything was home grown.
Now junk and fast food makes our stomachs groan.
Remember when gas and groceries were affordable to buy
Now smile and thank you and smack you right in the eye.

Oh yes that was way back then, those were the days.
Don't you think that everything today is out of phase?

A Large Plot of Ground

In New York City there is a large plot of ground.
It appears that it is destined to be permanent,
with Emptiness & Void.

Once on that very same ground there were
two beautiful handsome Giants, who used to stand ever
so proud and tall.

Miss Liberty raised her glowing torch to them, as if to
say, "See, we are the great ones people look up to, Ever so
tall,

See how proud we stand as we touch the heavens.

Yes my children we are the symbols of America.

We face the mighty storms that cross our paths.

People would use us for their advantage as we cradled
them for protection.

They would brag and boast how beautiful we are.
But within minutes on a gloomy saddened day the two
giants were wrenching with fires and heat that was too
unbearable for them.

My two children were finally beaten down to the ground.

Tears rolled down my cheeks. They are gone forever.

"Are we to be beaten, Have we been weaken by this
horrible event.

"Shouldn't we at least try to erect our 2 beautiful fallen
Giants as they once were?."

"As I look out from the bay I see emptiness."

And that my friends is how our lady, the Statute of
Liberty Sees It.

Written by JBS - 8/16/2008

Back To School and All The Crazies

This happened to me on my 1st day of school.
It that took place in 1933 at 5 years of age

It was supposed to be easy
But it turned out to be sleazy.

All my times were to be happy,
But it turned out to be wacky.

Times in my life I do not mention,
In school I was put in detention.

My very first day going to school,
At 5 years old there was no rule.

I threw a pumpkin at a store window glass
And the teacher whipped my Ass.

I was immediately sent to the principle's room.
And in turn she flogged me with her broom.

I laughed at her, I felt no pain
But all that punishment was not in vain.

Then she put her ruler to the palm of my hand.
She counted 1, 2, 3, 4 as if leading a band.

She pinned a note on my winter coat,
I was proud as can be with that note.

I was the only kid who had a teacher's letter,
I went home like a peacock and I felt better.

But when my father read it, he got so mad
He tried to kick me, slipped on the ice, I was glad.

Life is supposed to be easy and nice.
Even when married and get sprinkled with rice.

It was supposed to easy as we all know
And if it isn't it will surely show.

We may laugh or we may cry.
Lets hope it gets better before I die.

How Much Is Too Much?
Eating - Dancing - Dating

We all had to grow up no matter what.
And we all had to get out of that same old rut.

Hanging out with our peers at the local sweet shope.
And dancing with gals at a school prom or hop.

We dated with our favorite boys or gals.
No matter what, they were the best of pals.

Couldn't get enough of staying out late.
Had to get home early and that made us hate.

Getting up in the morning to go to school.
Without education we would turn into a fool.

Sometimes we would eat everything in site.
And that mom yell with all her might.

If we ate too much we would get round and fat.
And if we ate less, we would be thin as a baseball bat.

Who's to say how much is too much and who's to rule
Our lives on each day as we attend school.

Our teachers and parents may yell,
If we don't straighten out we may go to hell.

How I Started A Toy Loan Store

In 1934, in the gloomy Depression Days,
So depressed that all the people were in a daze.
I had an idea that was churning in my mind
Off to the junk store treasures I would find.
It doesn't pay to rob a store or does it?
If your intentions are good you may not get hit.
So I filled my pockets with junky old toys.
You know, boys will be boys
I only wanted to borrow just a little bit.
But when the owner saw me, he had a fit.
I was only taking a little bit here & a little bit there,
But when I got caught it really wasn't fair.
Mom & Dad had no money to spend on me,
I guess the parts & pieces I took were not meant to be.
It was only a 2nd hand store that people sold junk to,
To raise a little cash in times that were so blue.
Well, the owner grabbed me and called a cop,
I told them I was taking the stuff home to my work shop.
That I was going to fashion the stuff I took
Into better looking toys, and I really wasn't a crook.
I was only going to give them away to poor little kids,
Whose mothers & fathers were on the skids.
Your intentions are from the heart my young lad,
And here I thought you was just a little beggar who was bad.
Hmmn said the owner, as he said with a friendly glance,
"Promise to be good & rob no more, I'll give you an advance."
"You are to open a "Toy Loan Shope" in the back of my store.
So honest children can borrow them for ever more."
My Mom & Pop are proud of me now
& I can always hear them say,
"Because of you, children can borrow toys
so they can be happy everyday."

Stop Raining On My Parade

A little black cloud follows me wherever I go.
Its lightning cracks and the winds sure blow.
Please Stop Raining On My Parade I beg of you.
But the little cloud has its own point of view.

If you think your day is all that nice,
I'll turn it into snow and ice.
So I'll rain on your parade to ruin your day,
Tomorrow or next week, I'll have my say.

Just like your shadow, I'll follow you around.
So stop your moaning and don't utter a sound.
It doesn't listen to my pleas so it ruins by day,
Can't even go outside to run and play.

When my friends see me coming, they run away
Cursing and yelling, this is what they say.
"Keep your cloud away from us, It's like an air raid,"
"And please keep it from Raining on our Parade."

Raining On Your Parade, that's what I do.
I'll make you sick and give you the "Flu."
So think of me as your conscious, your black cloud,
Who Rains On Your Parade as I shout good and loud.

Some days I'll be there, some days I will not.
But really, do you really think I forgot...
To Rain On Your Parade when you're having fun?
Just remember, I'll be there keeping you on the run.

Stealing

An invitation is like and invitation to stealing.
When at a party, the food is sure appealing.

Just look at that table with all that cake and candy.
No one's looking so I'll pocket some, I feel dandy.

Everyone else is helping them selves, their eating too.
But I still feel like stealing, what else can I do.

Even if its free I feel the guilt, why do I feel this way?
I'm just as hungry as everyone else, so what can I say.

When I go out to dine, I steal the menu, why I don't know.
When in a store, I look around, no one's looking so here I go.

I didn't plan my life this way to steal goodies that are loose.
I don't care if I get caught or they hang me in noose.

Sometime I feel guilty and sometimes I feel mad
And if I don't steal It will the worse day I ever had.

Steal, steal, with all that money I'll have a house built.
And I'll do it without any remorse or guilt..

If someone out there listening me, help me please.
For I'm begging you on my bruised humble knees.

If I Could Fly

If I could fly, I would like to be an Eagle.
Not like a little dog, meaning the Beagle.

If I could run like lightning speed.
I know I can beat an Arabian Steed.

If I could, I should of, I would of maybe I can
Cool a house down like a huge electrical fan.

Lots of wishing goes into If only I could,
To become a giant redwood where I once stood.

If I could turn into a genie and with his magic
Make life here on earth and not so tragic.

If I could fly like that fat jolly old man
I would sprinkle happiness all over the land.

If I could, I wish I would, I'd put on a happy face
I would smile all the time, here, now, or any place.

If I could, maybe stopping the war would be nice.
Stopping crime, corruption and all that dopey vice.

If I could, yeah, I sure would with all this dreaming.
Stop gasoline from rising, with all their scheming.

If I could do a lot to help my fellow man
I would help as much as I possibly can.

I'm only one person, but if all people thought my way
They could change this world for the better some day.

If I could go on and on, wishing for a better life,
I would like to go through it with my pretty wife.

My First Pony Ride

The year was 1935, I was only 7 years old at the time. My cousin Richard & I were the same age. We were playing outside on Mary Street in front of Richard's house. His family was inside the house just visiting, talking & having a good time just like old folks like to do. Richard said, "Hey look Junior!"

Coming down the street was a beautiful tan & white Shetland pony with a white flowing tail, beautiful mane, with a brown leather studded saddle & with sparkling rhinestones. The man leading the pony was a photographer & yelling out "Have you picture taken with a cowboy suit with pistols & all on the pony for only 25 cents. (Pretty cheap in those days.)

The guy grabbed me & put me on the pony. I screamed bloody murder. My first pony ride was a catastrophe. He immediately took me off. I was still crying. I stood there just looking. What's all the hellabaloo about as my relatives came out of the house yelling. The photographer explained that he was only trying to set a photo shoot of me on the pony.

"Well if he doesn't want to get on the pony, don't force him." Just then Richard said, "I'll get on him & ride him." So now my cousin has a nice photograph of him on the pony & I have a bad experience of me on the pony. I was a cry baby. And to this day horses and I don't mix. So in my jealous rage, I picked up a tin can & threw it at Richard & it cut his nose.
He has a scar on the left side of his nose.

I ran away as fast as I could, no one saw me throw the can, but my guilt is still with me to this day. Richard has left this earth, maybe he is still riding the pony in "Heaven," that is.

The Strangest Thing

The strangest thing that ever happened to me was the night I was hypnotized.

I went to a late show that was put on by a hypnotist.

I volunteered to up on the stage and participate to be under the spell by the hypnotist. I wasn't alone on the stage, there others who wanted to participate.

I say that there were about 5 people besides myself.

Each one of was to be hypnotized by the hypnotist.

He put each one of us in a deep, deep sleep.

Then he made each one of us perform like a complete idiot on the stage.

Like one was a dog, a foolish person or some kind of crazy people antics.

He said when we woke up, we wouldn't remember a thing. And to this day I still can't remember.

I thought that was kind of strange.

I usually have great memory recall, but this time I couldn't remember a thing.

How did I know about the people and I doing stupid on the stage after they hypnotized?

My friends who were in the audience told me what had happened. It was hard to believe.

They said I was the dog who was barking and rolling all over the stage.

Maybe that is why when I see a dog today, I bark at it and start wagging my tail. Ha!...Kind of a nutty tail, huh?

That was a while back about in late 50s.

Call Me!
I Can't Remember Right Now!

I have a mind that's not my own,
Sometimes it feels all alone.
It slips away from its' way of thinking,
And it keeps my eyeballs a blinking.
Call me! I can't remember right now!
I feel I have a brain of a cow.
I have a telephone and I have a cell.
I can't remember why, pray tell.
In my note book, I jot things down.
I look them up and with a frown,
Can't remember why I wrote them down,
Makes me feel like a silly old clown.
Call me! I can't remember right now!
I feel like a fat old sow, rubbing my sweaty brow.
There must be a reason for everything I write,
I try to think of them with all my might.
Call me! I can't remember this night,
Is there to be no end in sight.
The phone is tingling and a ringing
It sounds like someone singing.
Hello, hello! are you calling me,
I can't remember right now you see
Please hang up, why did you call
I can't remember after all,
This ringing in my brain gets in the way
And I really have nothing to say.
But please call me! I can't remember right now!
But if you do, I'll try to remember why & how.

2 Face People

Jealously is the seeds of a 2 face,
It grows and grows at a steady pace.
One side is a happy face fancied with lots of lace,
While the other side is evil and filled with mace.

My father used to say to my mother after some of her friends came to visit, after leaving, he said, "They are two face," all they want from you is to cart them around town in your car and not to mention the handouts, meaning money you give them."

"They give you roses in front of you while behind your back they dig in their thorns. They are just using you."

My mom was an easy going beautiful person and she would say, "They are my friends, what am I can do?" "I love them all"

All through my life I heard the saying "Two Face." One side smiles as the other is sad, angry and jealous.

It's like the theatrical clown's face depicting comedy and tragedy. Life goes on no matter who ever our friends are, Some may be close to our hearts, while other remain cleverly afar.

But keep this in mind, choose wisely,
And weed out the bad one.
There could be one in your family,
maybe a daughter or even a son.

It's Free

After reading the newspapers,
Listening to the daily news on the TV,
Talking to relatives & many close friends,
Buying gas,
Groceries,
Paying rent.
All my many bills,
Doctors Fees,
Co-Payments,
Postage stamps,
Sampling free samples
at the Grocery Stores,
You hardly get enough anyway
and some taste really terrible.
Yea, sure it's free. They want you to buy, buy, buy!
The only thing I have to say with that Malarkey is...

What?

The old saying is, "You pay for what you get my friends."
And 2 things you have to do in life is pay taxes and die.

So remember my friends, next time they say it's FREE!,
Scratch your head and shout....**What?**

Oh Yeah, It's FREE,

They mean the Bird and the Bee.

Whiskey and Wild Red Indians Halloween

Give a bottle or bottles of that delicious whiskey or the
so called fire water to a wild bunch of Indians and you'll
see them all turn 4 or 5 deeper shades of crimson red.
And if that ain't enough & if there is enough to go around
you'll see them all dancing crazy & wild around the fires
under the moonlit desert skies as the coyotes howl.

Dancing to that crazy beat of the tom tom,
swaying side to side
10 Drunken Red Little Indians are dressed
with feathers & hide.
The cemetery close by is raising
its dead from all the noise it hears
The ghouls are awakening from the
banging ringing in their ears.
It's like a Halloween scene that comes to life
just because of that firery whiskey
And all the Indians & kids from all over join in,
it makes them feel pretty frisky.
Have a drink of that punch that is punched
with the scented flavorful fume.
Their kidneys weaken and the relief of
fulfillment will make the flowers bloom.
Now the painted desert looks like it should
because of that colored petrified wood.
Whiskey, Red Indians, Kids, Ghouls, Spooks,
Cemeteries & Halloween really do mix.
So if you see a glowing bottle of that fire water,
pick it up, have a guzzle & get a fix.

Tom The Turkey, Tom The Holiday Bird

"Gobble, gobble, gobble,"
said Tom the Turkey, As he walk with a wobble.
If you burst my bubble, I'll be in trouble.

Put that axe away like they do at the White House,
If you do I'll promise to be quiet as a mouse.
You can't get me on that plate,
But if you do, that will be my fate.

I'm stuffed up to the gill. So say grace and be very still,
Then you can eat me, & have your fill.
Would you like my wing or my drum stick?
Have some stuffing, have your pick.

Or would you prefer me as a chicken.
Gravy is on your finger, you'll be a'licken.
When your all done with me there will be my bones
Then you can cover me with dirt and stones.

I'll fly away with my wings on the wind
From the coup, that's where I've been.
So have a Happy Thanksgiving Day
And remember me to this way.

Next time you decide to eat me and have your fill,
I'll chase you all around and peck you with my bill.
For I am Tom the Turkey, the holiday bird,
Ain't this the craziest story you ever heard?

Christmas Parade

The children got out of bed all by themselves without be told. They are behaving especially well today.

They brushed their teeth, washed behind their ears they even made their beds.

The children are so excited because today is the Christmas parade.
They didn't have to be told to come to the table for breakfast.

The Christmas Tree was all spruced up and the twinkling lights reminded them that the parade was ready to start.

The sleigh was in front of the house decorated with colors of red and green lights, golden sleigh bells which would peal off the cadence of the waiting reindeers.

Santa was ready for the happy event all dressed up in his red colorful suit that Mrs. Claus made for him. The elves came along for the ride.

The new fallen snow on the ground would made for a smooth easy gliding sleigh.

"Come On Kids," said Santa and Bring your mother and father too...Oooops, I forgot, that's us, all dressed up in red & white." "Don't forget your elf hats."

"Let's celebrate the Christmas Spirit and have fun in the parade today. You can toss the candies and presents to the children who don't have much. That's what Christmas is all about. Giving & Sharing, isn't that a warm & pleasant thought?

"Are you all ready? Hang on, here we go." With a snap of a make - believe whip, the reindeer were off led by of course, Rudolph, the red nose fellow.

Everyone was shouting "Merry Christmas to all and to all a happy ride on this day of the "Christmas Parade."

Leaves

It is Autumn, make way for the falling leaves.
Colored by Nature's palate of boundless hues.
The air is cold but refreshing & just right for hiking.
Colored leaves are shimmering by the cold brisk winds.
They dance in the air as they float to the ground.
They hated to say "Goodbye" to their held fast branches.
Mother earth is very happy to coddle them in her bosom.

The uneven mounds of painted delights are moved briskly as they swirl around like the sand dunes of a painted desert.

The forests are so pleasing to the eye, the vibrant colors are ever so breathless to feast upon. We devour them with amazement & understanding..

The rolling hills are like living colored carpets put down by Nature's gentle hand.

She is an awesome lady with a magical touch of genius like painters of old, but still reminding them she was here first, then the painters came to imitate her with their hand made brushes.

What is so magical about a leaf, colored or not, that floats to the ground?

Is it part of life that detaches itself from the living giant of a woodland tree?

Just like humans do when they were born to this earth and also are detached.

Our eyes and mind like pleasing things to watch and we are awed by the leaf.

It reminds of everlasting emittance of like itself.

It sprouts out to gather the energy of the sun but later dies from exhaustion.

Then it gently floats to earth where it will forever rest.

On The Farm

As a youngster, one could say, I grew up on a farm or should I say farmlands.

In the summertime, when school was let out, I used to go bean picking with my aunt Josephine, I used to call her "Zizzie". Here face and hands were very tanned skin from the sun. Boy could she fill a bushel of beans fast. She was from Naples, Italy and was used to this kind of life. She came from the farm hills and always had a garden with all kinds of vegetables.

Early in the mornings around 6 a.m., a large truck would pick up the pickers waiting in front of there houses and haul us to the country's farmland. The ride was 1 hr or so.

We would pick pole beans or peas, depending on the owner of the farm. I seen more farms that you can imagine. Old farms with the traditionally Red Barn and leaning silos from the strong winds that sometimes blew the lid off some of them.

As teenagers, my buddies & I would go back to some of the farms and ask the owner if we could hunt woodchucks. Very seldom were we refused. Those varmints were always digging holes on the farm & horses would break their legs if one got caught in one of them.

My family's very first formal visit was to a friend of my father called Links. The farm was somewhere near Richfield Springs, N.Y. near Cooperstown, N.Y.

I never had such delicious food in my life. All the food was fresh, picked of the vines. the meats were butchered on the farm. I was the greatest eating experience in my life.

How well I remembered the Swiss Chard just picked out of the garden and cooked, it was so tender, I never tasted anything like it. There is no comparison to the veggies that you buy in the today's stores. That is probably why I married Dolores, who was raised on a quaint farm in Richfield Springs on Montecello road.

Good Times

My childhood days were the good times in my life. My mother and father would bring my sister and I hot fudge sundaes when they went out dancing Saturday nights. My sister baby sat me, there were no problems.

Daytime, we would go the the "Power Dam", Utica's popular swimming area. All the neighborhood would be there. My friends and I would swim and play. every family picked a parking spot and there they would picnic. Hot dogs, hamburgers, soft drinks and whatever else that was needed to make for happy days.

It was there I learned how to swim. My father, while holding, would teach me how to tread water and then let go, I would be on my own. I was swimming solo. They were great times.

Later in the evening we would drive to an Ice Cream Drive In. It seemed that the whole city was there getting there favorite Ice cream cones. My favorite flavor was black cherry walnut. Yummy, yum, yum.

My father and I would toboggan down the local ski slope. after all tired he would set me on the toboggan and pull me all the way home. My mother was waiting for us with hot chicken and biscuits smothered with gravy. As I got older, I would do the same things on my own.

After getting married I would do the same things with my wife and 4 daughters. I would take them to Sylvan Beach, called Oneida Lake. We would watch the barges come in via the Erie Canal and Mohawk river.

Then we would take in the carnival, ferris wheel, have some cotton candy. Many years later we would visit the white church that was popular for movie making.